H M Co

EUROPE

At the request of

John L. Rikhoff

of Africa,

Far East

Houghton Mifflin Company has
provided this examination copy for
your professional consideration.
In making this book available for
your study we are reaffirming our
belief that teachers and textbooks
are the two most important influences in education at all levels.

List Price $ 1 95

HOUGHTON MIFFLIN COMPANY
MIDWESTERN DIVISION
GENEVA, ILLINOIS

D1207630

THE WORLD
BEYOND EUROPE

*An Introduction to the History of Africa,
India, Southeast Asia, and the Far East*

GEORGE ALEXANDER LENSEN
The Florida State University

HOUGHTON MIFFLIN COMPANY • BOSTON
The Riverside Press Cambridge

To Karen
who had crossed the Pacific
before she was two

The Riverside Press
CAMBRIDGE, MASSACHUSETTS

PRINTED IN THE U. S. A.

PREFACE

The world beyond Europe entered the ken of European history relatively late. Western civilization textbooks touch upon it primarily in the Age of Exploration, the Age of Imperialism, and the period since the Russo-Japanese War. They view it as a mirror in which European voyages and rivalries are reflected. It is the purpose of this book to add another dimension to the traditional chapters by sketching in the histories of the regions to which the Westerners ventured and in which the ways of life were not supplanted by the civilization of Europe, or, more broadly, of the West. The book has been arranged in such a way as to supplement most effectively the standard histories of Western civilization. The threefold division facilitates not only the assignment of "parallel reading" in college classes but also the orientation of the general reader, who is shown the world beyond Europe from familiar vantage points. Considerations of space have dictated the exclusion of the Near East, which generally receives some coverage in textbooks of Western civilization.

Chinese and Japanese names are given in the traditional order — family name first. Chinese names are romanized according to the Wade-Giles system. The apostrophe indicates that the preceding consonant is "soft"; a consonant not followed by an apostrophe is "hard." For example, "Ch'in" is pronounced like the English word "chin"; "Chin" like the English word "gin"; "Taoism" as if it were spelled with a "D."

I am indebted to Professor William E. H. Howard of the Florida Agricultural and Mechanical University, to Professors

Charles H. Fairbanks and Wallace W. Reichelt of the Florida
State University, to Professor Benjamin Franklin Rogers Jr.,
Vice-President of Jacksonville University, and to Dr. Harbans
S. Puri of the Florida Geological Survey, for reading parts of the
manuscript and making helpful suggestions. I am grateful also
for the splendid editorial assistance of Mr. Henry F. Thoma and
Miss Eleanor Wiles of Houghton Mifflin Company. Responsi-
bility for what I have written rests solely with me. I thank the
Princeton University Press for permitting me to draw on some
passages from my book, *The Russian Push Toward Japan; Russo-
Japanese Relations, 1697–1875* (Princeton, 1959).

G. A. L.

Tallahassee, Florida
January, 1960

CONTENTS

MAPS

CHART

PART ONE

IN THE AGE OF EXPLORATION

AFRICA

Until the construction of the Suez Canal in the second half of the nineteenth century, the giant continent of Africa lay athwart the sea lanes from Europe to the Far East. In the days of Marco Polo and before, Westerners had reached China overland. But the disintegration of the Mongol empire made the land routes unsafe, and the new monarchies of the Atlantic states, weary of Mediterranean and Arabic middlemen, turned seaward to find their own way to the East. Step by step they groped their way down the coast of Africa and at last, in the fifteenth century, spearheaded by the Portuguese, rounded the Cape of Good Hope and discovered the way to India.

The Africa which the Europeans touched in the Age of Exploration was not a country or a seat of common culture but a massive continent, the second largest in the world, about 11,700,000 square miles or roughly three times the size of Europe in extent. Predominantly a plateau, higher in the south than in the north, with steep drops along the edges down to the narrow coastal plains, Africa lies mostly (eighty per cent) in the tropics.

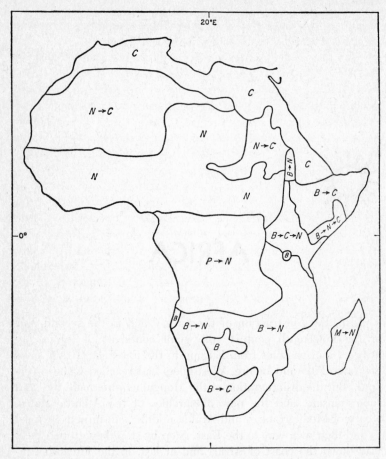

DISTRIBUTION OF RACES IN AFRICA

KEY: N, Negroid; B, Bushmanoid; P, Pygmoid; M, Mongoloid; C, Caucasoid

From J. P. Murdock, *Africa: Its People and Their Cultural History;* copyright, 1959, McGraw-Hill Book Co., Inc.

The vast expanse of the continent and the differences in elevation entail considerable variation in humidity and temperature, however. The elevated plateau regions, rising to an average height of two thousand feet above the equatorial jungles and swamps at sea level, are relatively cool and healthful.

The population, believed to have numbered about 75,000,000 in 1500 (almost fifty per cent greater than that of Europe), was notable no less for its diversity than its size. There were five prominent racial strains — Negroid, Bushmanoid, Pygmoid, Mongoloid, and Caucasoid — ranging in skin color from black to yellowish-brown, yellow, and white. Of these, the Negroid and the Caucasoid had gained dominance, the former occupying the bulk of the continent, the latter the shores of the Mediterranean and a few other coastal fringes. The Sahara, a desert zone about three thousand miles in length and a thousand in width, was a far more effective barrier between northern Africa and the rest of the continent than was the Mediterranean Sea between northern Africa and southern Europe. The Sahara was, generally speaking, the natural dividing line between "white" and "black" Africa. Beyond the Sahara the continental dominance of the "blacks" reached back to ancient times, when Bantu and other Negro tribes of relatively large build, with a knowledge of pastoral and agricultural economy, pushed down from the Sudan to intermingle with or displace the Negrillos — the Pygmies, Bushmen, and Hottentots — of the south.

A look at a map will readily reveal Africa's ancient points of contact with Asia and Europe. In the northeast corner, where Africa is now severed from Eurasia by the Suez Canal, a strip of land joined the continents and blocked passage from the Mediterranean to the Red Sea. Further south, the Red Sea narrowed, and the Arabian peninsula and Africa swung toward each other to within easy crossing distance. Finally, the Mediterranean itself, an inland sea but for the narrow strait at its western end that separated Africa from Spain, bound southern Europe and northern Africa to a common Mediterranean culture.

Ancient Egypt is commonly regarded as one of the roots of the European heritage. Its story is included in most histories of Western civilization and, therefore, need not be retold here. Cradled in the Nile river region, in northeast Africa, the Egyptian realm at the height of its power (about 1450 B.C.) extended its military might southward into what is now the Sudan; commercially it stretched out to East Africa as well as westward, along the Mediterranean coast.

It was along the shores of northern Africa, too, in modern Tunisia, that Phoenician traders established themselves as early as the twelfth century B.C. In the ninth century the Phoenicians founded an African colony, Carthage, near the site of modern Tunis. Ultimately Carthage came to dominate all of northwest Africa, and in the third century B.C. her armies, under the great Carthaginian general Hannibal, seriously threatened the power of Rome. The Phoenicians extended their knowledge of Africa far beyond the areas of their control. They navigated from Egypt down the east coast, around the cape and up the west coast, some two thousand years before Vasco da Gama, the Portuguese explorer, rounded the cape from the opposite direction.

Meanwhile, in the seventh century B.C., Greek settlements had sprouted in Africa. Wedged between Egypt and Carthage, they formed the region of Cyrenaica, so called after Cyrene, the leading Greek city in Africa. The celebrated historian Herodotus, the "Father of History," visited North Africa in the fifth century, and spread among his Greek countrymen whatever he had been able to learn about the continent. The Greeks penetrated also into Egypt, but in the sixth and fifth centuries Egypt fell under Persian rule, until conquered by Alexander the Great in the fourth century. The city of Alexandria, which Alexander founded in 332 B.C., became the center of the Hellenistic empire, which embraced not only Egypt, Syria, Palestine, and Asia Minor, but at one time extended all the way to India.

In the first century B.C. the Romans defeated Carthage and organized its territories into a Roman province, Africa Proconsularis. From this, the name "Africa" came to be applied to the whole continent. Native states to the west were eventually annexed to the province, as were the Greek settlements to the east and Egypt. With North Africa part of the Roman Empire, the Mediterranean Sea became a Roman lake, across which African foodstuffs moved to Europe, and Graeco-Roman civilization and, in time, Christianity to Africa. Ethiopia (Abyssinia), an inde-

pendent state whose dynasty traced its lineage back to King
Solomon and the Queen of Sheba, and which in the past had
had contacts with Egyptians, Greeks, and Jews, became the
bulwark of African Christendom.

The division of the Roman Empire in 395 A.D. entailed the
split-up of North Africa. Egypt and Cyrenaica, predominantly
Greek in speech, became part of the Byzantine Empire. The
rest of North Africa did not remain in Western Roman hands
for long. In 429 A.D. it was overrun by the Vandals, who thereby
deprived the empire of its "breadbasket" and hastened its demise.
But the Vandals in turn were defeated by Byzantine forces, and
North Africa was reunited as part of the Eastern Roman Empire.

In the seventh century A.D., Egypt, Ethiopia, and the coastal
areas of North Africa were conquered by the Arabs and fellow
Moslems. When Spain and Sicily suffered the same fate, the way
was opened for the introduction into Africa of Spanish (Roman)
as well as Moslem culture, the latter embodying Hellenistic and
Persian concepts. Penetrating ever deeper into the interior —
southward up the Nile river into the Sudan, and westward
through the desert into Nigeria — the Arabs extended their influence.

Unable to gain a permanent foothold in Europe, the Arabs
and their Turk coreligionists succeeded in perpetuating their
position in North Africa until the nineteenth century, disseminat-
ing their Islamic faith and culture. The role of the Berbers, the
white natives of northwest Africa, with whom the Arabs inter-
married, was not passive. Hand in hand with the Arabs, they
developed a remarkable Arabic-Berber (Moorish) civilization,
which surpassed medieval Europe in scientific knowledge and
learning. Indeed, it was in the Moslem schools and courts of
Spain and North Africa that Christian students developed the
geographical knowledge and scientific approach associated with
the modern era.

Using the camel, and activated by missionary zeal, the Arabs
pushed deep into Africa. They did not bring political unity to
the continent, for rival Moslem dynasties — the Fatimite, Almora-
vide, Almohade, and others — were competing with each other;

but they left a greater imprint on Africa than previous invaders. Berbers who wished to escape Arab restrictions in the north moved into the western Sudan, spreading Arabic-Berber culture among the darker peoples. In the eleventh century, when the Normans took Sicily, Tunisia, and Tripoli, and Arab power in Spain crumbled, the Berbers took the initiative in military and cultural expansion, spreading Arabic-Berber civilization among the inhabitants of the Senegal and Niger river valleys in the west.

New states and cities had come into being in various parts of Africa by this time. Along the east coast, between the Limpopo and Zambesi rivers, there were several small Moslem states, collectively known as the Zenji empire. In this region, notably at Zimbabwe (modern Rhodesia), which had trade relations with places as distant as Sung China, ruins of a high civilization have been discovered, but it is not clear whether this civilization was native, Arabic, Phoenician, or, as is most likely, a combination of the three.

In the Sudan there were several native kingdoms of note: Ghana, Melle, Bornu, and Songhay. They were remarkably prosperous, because the Sudan, until the discovery of America, was one of the major sources of gold. At Kumbi Saleh, which is believed to have been the site of Ghana's capital (a twin city consisting of a royal city and a nearby Moslem merchant city), remnants of an advanced civilization have been excavated, including such iron products as nails, farming tools, knives, scissors, lances, and arrowheads, as well as glass weights and fragments of Mediterranean pottery. The merchant city, it is now estimated, measured about a square mile in area and numbered some thirty thousand inhabitants. The kingdom of Melle or Mali was no less civilized and prosperous. There, women, though Moslem, were more honored than men and walked about unveiled. When Kankan Musa, the celebrated ruler of Melle, made a pilgrimage to Mecca in 1325, he is said to have been accompanied by five hundred slaves, each holding a golden staff about six pounds in weight.

The Sudanese kingdom of Songhay became dominant in the sixteenth century under the able rule of Askia the Great. Administered well and governed by law, Songhay was notable also for its impressive architecture and manufactures of leather, iron, and tin. Its celebrated city of Timbuktu, founded at the bend of the Niger river in the eleventh century, rocketed to fame as a center of trade in gold, slaves, and salt, and as a showplace of African civilization. Prosperous gathering place of Moslem merchants and intellectuals from distant regions, Timbuktu boasted a university of Koranic studies at the mosque of Sankoré, a Moslem cathedral. "In Timbuktu," Leo Africanus reported, "there are numerous judges, doctors, and clerics, all receiving good salaries from the king. He pays great respect to men of learning. There is a big demand for books in manuscript, imported from Barbary. More profit is made from the book trade than from any other line of business." Ironically, Timbuktu was destroyed not by Westerners but by fellow Moslems, the Moors. Indirectly, European explorations contributed to its downfall. As long as the Moslems had served Europe as indispensable middlemen, trading African and Far Eastern products for European wares, they had prospered in relative peace. But once the Europeans found their own way to the East, they excluded the "infidels" from Europe, thereby driving them to take by force what they no longer could obtain by commerce. The Moors preyed on Christian shipping on the one hand and crushed the Moslem African kingdom of Songhay (1591) on the other. Sudanese Africa, now cut off from the rest of the world, became culturally stagnant. But the destruction of Songhay benefited the Moors little. Their own state, Morocco, and their own Moorish civilization, continued to decline.

With increased penetration into Africa, Moslem knowledge of the continent advanced. The celebrated traveler Ibn Battuta recorded his impressions of North Africa and the east coast down to Kilwa in the fourteenth century, and Leo Africanus his travels in the Sudan in the sixteenth. Although the observations of Leo Africanus, a Moor who had been captured by Christian pirates and given to the pope, were published in 1563 (translated into English in 1600), Europeans were not generally acquainted with the high moral and intellectual writings of their African

and Arabic-Berber contemporaries. Nor did they have any direct contact with the civilizations of the continent. Along the
Atlantic shores, where the Portuguese landed, primitive tribes
shielded the advanced civilizations from discovery. Thus the
Westerners in the Age of Exploration knew nothing of the tremendous camel caravans that crossed the desert annually. They
had no idea that cannon had been used in battle in Africa half
a century earlier than in Europe, or that the royal palace in
Ghana had windows of glass. They little suspected that civilizations not inferior to their own had flourished south of the Sahara
for some three centuries. To be sure, these civilizations, like most,
were partly foreign in stimulus, but that did not detract from
their significance. Moreover, though the historical rediscovery of
Africa is still, in our own day, far from complete, the findings
of archaeologists and scholars suggest more "native" elements in
these cultures than has hitherto been realized.

The economy of Africa, when the Europeans arrived, was
predominantly agricultural in the central portion of the continent,
pastoral in the northern and southwestern portions, with regions
of a mixed agricultural and pastoral economy, and islands of
remnant hunters here and there. When they first reached Africa,
the Portuguese built forts and trading posts along the Guinea
coast. Later they dislodged the Arabs from the ports on the
eastern coast and transferred their activities to that side of the
continent. They penetrated also inland to modern Rhodesia,
and were influential in Ethiopia. Their flourishing trade in
slaves, gold, spices, and ivory attracted adventurers from other
parts of Europe. In the seventeenth century the Dutch, and in
the eighteenth and nineteenth centuries the French and English,
encroached on their acquisitions.

The traffic in Negro slaves was not a European innovation.
Both native rulers and Arab traders had engaged in it for many
years. But with the arrival of the Portuguese it reached staggering proportions. Craving for Western products, African chiefs
sold fellow Africans, sometimes their own subjects, to the European merchants. One common way of obtaining slaves was to
set fire to a settlement at night and grab the frantic inhabitants

as they tried to flee to safety. So great was the general demoralization which the slave trade fostered that parents sold their own children to the foreigners. Over the years literally millions of Africans were torn from their homes. Countless were those who perished in transit; countless those who suffered in bondage. It has been estimated, moreover, that only about fifty per cent of the natives dragged from Africa survived to become fully usable slaves.

Meanwhile native society within Africa was utterly disrupted. The advanced kingdoms of medieval Africa disappeared before the inland incursions of the Europeans. Perhaps already devitalized by dynastic wars, they suffered economic ruin when the Europeans took control of the coasts and dislocated the patterns of trade. There still existed coastal cities which impressed the Portuguese favorably with their level of culture, but on the whole the Africans who were subjected to the Western impact were primitive farmers leading a communal life of collectivism. African society was dominated by the tribal system, each tribe ruled by a tribal chief, each settlement by a local chief. There were chiefs who had become arbitrary despots, but as a rule the authority of the chief was limited. He could not make laws, for the tribal life was regulated by customs. Whatever administrative latitude he had within the framework of customs, he was to exercise in consultation with his councillors. The people of Africa were not prepared to take in stride the sudden change in pace, indeed the completely different outlook, brought by the Westerners, especially in later years, after the Industrial Revolution. They were not able to adjust themselves in a brief span of time to the rigors of an urban, industrial, individualistic society, an adjustment that had taken centuries to effect in Europe under far more favorable and natural conditions.

The British and the French concentrated on West Africa; the Dutch entrenched themselves in the south, where they founded the Cape settlement. But Western knowledge of the continent remained scanty. Until the middle of the nineteenth century Africa remained to Europeans little more than a series of coastlines. Where Europeans did penetrate inland to the complex

African kingdoms, they destroyed them in order to monopolize trade, just as they did in India and Peru. The prime importance of Africa in the Age of Exploration, other than as a source of slaves and gold, lay in its position as steppingstone in Europe's path to the East.

INDIA

The historical contacts of the "West" with the "East" date back to pre-Christian times. In the sixth century B.C. the forces of Darius I penetrated to the Indus plain and made western Punjab a province of the Persian empire, drawing cotton-clad troops, war elephants, and tribute in gold from this, their richest and most populous satrapy. In 326 B.C. Alexander the Great, in his conquest of the Persian domains, crossed the Indus river over a bridge of boats, and continuing eastward overran the Indian armies, whose chariots and elephants, however impressive in appearance, were like sitting ducks to the highly mobile Greek cavalry and mounted infantry. But unlike the sway of the Persians, who retained western Punjab for a century and a half, Greek rule was shortlived. A mutiny of his troops, who had been separated from their homeland for eight years, forced Alexander to halt his advance before reaching the Ganges plain and head back to Europe. The garrisons he left behind remained only a few years, Alexander's early death (323 B.C.) precipitating the break-up of the vast Macedonian empire.

In the days of Persian domination, Greeks and Indians seem to have visited each other's lands and to have exchanged philosophical views. In the days of Alexander, an Indian ascetic made his way to Babylon and there burned himself to death. But though Alexander had plans of Hellenizing India and might have built another Alexandria at the mouth of the Indus river had he lived longer, and though we can discern some Hellenic influence in Buddhist sculpture and painting, his intrusion, ignored in ancient Indian writings, was quite limited in impact. In Roman times a flourishing sea trade developed with southern India by way of Alexandria and the Red Sea, the Suez isthmus being negotiated by journeys overland or via the Nile river canals. But though Roman colonies were planted in southern India, their influence too was only ephemeral. It was not until the close of the fifteenth century A.D. — in 1498, to be exact — that the relative isolation, in which the major cultures of the world had been developing more or less independently, was truly broken by the arrival of Vasco da Gama with three Portuguese vessels at the coast of India.

The India which the Portuguese "discovered" was not a country or a nation, but a subcontinent, over a million and a half square miles in extent. Covering an area roughly the size of Europe minus Russia, India was a mosaic of different peoples. Racially there were many divisions, subdivisions, and mixtures, extending all the way from black to white, and incorporating Mongoloid elements. There was no less of a range in level of cultural development, embracing the most primitive and also the most cultured groups. Linguistically there were fifteen major tongues and over a hundred and fifty minor ones, not counting dialects. The very name "India" is a Western appellation, derived from the river Indus (Sindhu), which created a breach in the mountain wall through which Alexander the Great and his Greek forces poured in the Hellenistic Age. "Hindustan," the term which the Indians themselves used, meant "Land of the Hindus," and referred to a limited area, at most to the whole northern plains region. There were other names, but the concept of India as a nation state with a common name, language, and

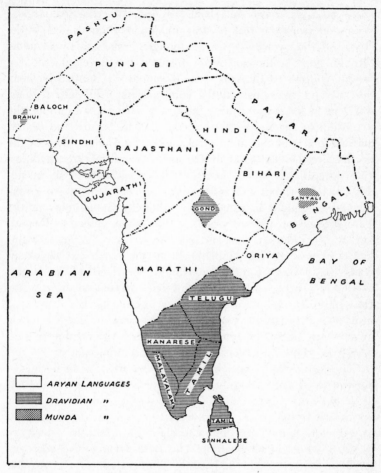

LINGUISTIC DIVISIONS IN INDIA

From H. G. Rawlinson, *India — A Short Cultural History;* copyright, 1952, Frederick A. Praeger Inc.

government was yet in the future, a byproduct, in a way, of the Western impact.

The diversity and disunity of India were rooted in the geography of the subcontinent. With its jutting triangular penin-

sula, India was more than half surrounded by the sea. It was
separated from the rest of Asia by a mountainous wall — the
"roof of the world" — which, though breached by invaders
through gaps in the northwest, fostered the development of a
unique culture. At the same time, formidable mountain barriers,
deserts, and rivers carved the subcontinent itself into regions,
different in language, culture, and race. Thus, for example, the
peninsula in the south, the Deccan plateau toward the center,
and the plains of the Indus river and of the Ganges river in the
north were the centers of diverse peoples and cultures, a difference accentuated by the fact that the inhabitants of the north,
descendants primarily of Indo-Aryans and Moslems, were generally tall and light in complexion, while the inhabitants of the
southern regions, primarily of the ethnic stock known as Dravid-
ian, were of darker skin and shorter stature. As invader followed invader through the breach in the northwest mountain
wall, the earlier intruders remained, deprived of a natural
avenue of escape, and the subcontinent's population became increasingly diverse and complex. The internal barriers were not
insurmountable, however, and geography was not the sole factor
in delaying unification until modern times. The residue of successive invasions long blocked the flow of national unity.

The India which the Portuguese found was the home of ancient civilizations. A highly advanced urban culture had existed
as early as the fourth millennium B.C. But it had left no lasting
imprint on history, and the diversity of India was the product
of the many dynasties, often of foreign origin, which had superseded this ancient civilization. The Indo-Aryans, who were related in language and perhaps to some extent in race to the
Persians, Greeks, Latins, and other peoples of Europe, moved
into the subcontinent about 2000 B.C. They gave India its classical language (Sanskrit) and its classical literature: religious
hymns (vedas), religious prose compositions (upanishads), and
epics (gitas). These influenced the religious outlook and artistic
expressions of later centuries, and constituted the foundations of
the Hindu tradition.

The Indo-Aryans were followed by Persian and Greek invaders in the sixth and fourth centuries B.C. But the first Indian empire was established by a native of the subcontinent, Chandragupta Maurya, in the fourth century B.C., shortly after Alexander's invasion and withdrawal. Chandragupta's grandson, King Asoka (died 232 B.C.), extended the sway of the Maurya from northern India to the Deccan plateau. He was one of the truly great leaders of world history, tempering politics with idealism, and becoming the Constantine of Buddhism. From the Maurya dynasty, which ended in 184 B.C., India inherited the memory of an autocratic state, whose power may have been undermined, however, by religious emphasis. There followed a centuries-long chaotic interlude of invasions by Asian nomads, during which the kingdoms of the south dominated the scene. Though less influential in the shaping of the Indian tradition and never in control of the north, the southern states too had an advanced civilization. Their relative distance and isolation from the waves of foreign invaders gave them a unique role in preserving Indian culture and in extending it to Southeast Asia.

In the fourth century A.D., India witnessed the establishment of the Gupta dynasty, the second native empire. Holding sway over most of northern India through the sixth century, the Gupta gave to their region (as Europe was entering the Dark Ages) an era that was economically prosperous. Hinduism and classical literature reached their height, and Buddhism moved from emphasis on individual effort to reliance on a savior. Art flourished, as did science and especially mathematics, the so-called "Arabic" numerals being of Indian origin.

Toward the end of the fifth century the nomadic White Huns and the Rajput tribes overran the Gupta domains. They affected the Indian tradition relatively little. Of greater consequence was the next wave of foreign invaders. By the end of the eighth century Turkish and Afghan Moslems had begun to penetrate the land, and by the thirteenth century the whole Indo-Gangetic region was in their hands. They were followed by other Moslems of Mongol and Turkish stock in the thirteenth and fourteenth centuries. In 1526 Babur, a Mongol descendant of Tamerlane and a Moslem by faith, founded the so-called Mogul (Mongol) dynasty, which ruled the greater part of India at the time of the arrival of the Europeans.

Unlike earlier invaders, the Moslems resisted assimilation to the Indian way of life; at the same time, they failed to displace Hinduism. Offended by the native idols and erotica, against which Islam inveighed, the iconoclastic Moslems wrought enormous damage; they destroyed works of art, architectural monuments, and religious writings (both Hindu and Buddhist), and plunged Indian thought into an abyss of stagnation. Though the Moslems brought to the subcontinent a grandiose architecture of their own, their contribution was outweighed by their destruction and, above all, by the heritage of religious cleavage and hatred between Moslems and Hindus, which they bequeathed to India. Though Akbar (reigned 1556–1605), the most distinguished emperor of the Mogul dynasty, sought to unite the subcontinent by means of a salaried civil service, uniform measures and weights, standardized taxes, and even a new religion (worked out by himself eclectically from the other faiths and thus, he hoped, acceptable to everyone), he could not overcome the profound divisions of Indian society.

Rooted in geography and history, Indian disunity was augmented by its religious heritage. Not only were there numerous religions — Brahmanism, Buddhism, Jainism, Sikhism, Parsiism, various tribal religions, Islam, and Christianity — but the major ones encompassed within themselves the most diverse beliefs.

Hinduism, the dominant complex of Indian thought and customs, and Brahmanism, its organized religious form, had no "revealed" scripture, no one bible, which tied Hindu adherents to a common body of doctrines and dogmas. Various forms of religion and philosophy, ranging from a primitive animism and polytheistic idol-worship to a deeply spiritual monotheism and philosophical monism, were equally part and parcel of the Hindu experience. The hymns of Indo-Aryan times were polytheistic. They spoke of many deities who, like their Greek counterparts, generally were personifications of natural forces. The religious prose writings, on the other hand, were monotheistic, envisaging an Absolute Being or World Soul. To some, Brahma, the personification of the world soul, was most meaningful; to the majority, Shiva, the deity of destruction, and Vishnu, the deity of preservation, in its manifold reincarnations, were more inspiring.

The Hindus saw human suffering as the byproduct of man's craving for worldly possessions and for the gratification of his physical desires. They believed that the soul (but not matter) was real and eternal, and that mere death could not free the individual from earthly suffering, as the soul would continue in another form. The objective of the wise man should therefore be to free himself from craving; to free himself from self; to attain what might be called selflessness (and thus nonbeing) by spiritual union with the world soul or the universe. This was a difficult and slow process that required, as a rule, more than one lifetime of understanding and striving. The Hindus envisaged an endless chain of existences, the fortunes in every life being determined by the individual's conduct in a previous existence.

In his early stage of development, according to Hindu belief, man had but the most primitive instincts and needs; he was but a serf. With time his ambition would increase, and he would strive for wealth; he would become a farmer or a merchant. As he learned that money is not everything, and put greater value on honor, he would attain the status of a soldier. Only after a long period of learning and reflection, after many existences, would he reach the wisdom of unattachment to physical and worldly cravings and objects, and attain to the ideal state of a priest (brahmin). These stages of man's development were formulated into the caste system, with serfs, farmers and merchants, soldiers and aristocrats, and priests forming the four main layers of society. The untouchables, or outcasts, remained outside and below the caste structure. Though possibly based on color at its inception, the Aryan invaders trying to preserve their racial identity and assert their superiority, the caste system thus assumed the function of a ladder in religious education.

As it solidified, the caste system, with its manifold subdivisions, became the socio-economic-religious skeleton of the Hindu way of life. A person was born into a particular caste, and could not move up socially. Indeed, he was born into one of the hundreds of sub-castes, which developed within the four main castes, and could not transgress their bounds. He could not marry outside his circle, and was hindered from social intercourse with members of other sub-castes by such barriers as strict dietary rules. He was born also into an economic niche, constrained to follow the particular trade of his caste, though this restriction was less rigid than the prohibition on intermarriage. The caste system had its good points. Within each sub-caste the individual found help and security. The Hindu way of life was not "negative," for the negation of material and physical aspirations was balanced by the belief that every soul was eternally part of the world soul and could be reunited with it. The implications of Hinduism were many. The disdain for worldly success was a factor which inhibited not only the systematic recording of transitory historical events — much of our knowledge of India comes from foreign sources — but "progress" in general. The Hindu concept of the transmigration of souls in human or animal form entailed the sanctity of all life, especially that of the cow (so important in attaining a pastoral economy in ancient times) and was to form the ethical basis of later nonviolence and pacifism. The Hindu view that men were unequal, in spirit, intellect, and general capacity, sanctioned not only the caste system, but standards relative to the individual's make-up. Believing that absolute truth was beyond ordinary man, and that different solutions might be "right" for different men, Hindu relativism blended eventually with pacifism into the neutralism of modern times, so irritating to men of the Judaeo-Christian tradition. But above all, though it gave everyone the security of group identity, the caste system accentuated and perpetuated differences, and constituted a formidable barrier to the unity of the Indian people.

Buddhism, the major vehicle of Indian influence on Southeast Asia and the Far East, was an offshoot of Hinduism. Like Jainism, it was born in the sixth century B.C. as a protest against the increasing power of the Hindu clergy, and the transformation of Hindu philosophy into a priesthood-ridden organized religion

(Brahmanism). Unlike Jainism, which leaned toward extreme asceticism, some followers starving themselves to death, Buddhism brought a message of moderation and hope. To be sure, Prince Siddharta Gautama (563–483 B.C.), the historical founder of Buddhism, also taught the rising above and renunciation of self, advocated by Hindu philosophers. On the other hand, he questioned the reality of the soul, both individual and universal; he regarded matter as real, but he stressed the impermanence of all things, and the process of change as the underlying principle. He saw human suffering as the result of man's frustration in seeking to raise and continue the self, which, like the soul, was but a mirage. Through selflessness, the chain of causation and rebirths (which Gautama still postulated) could be broken, and peace and the end of suffering attained.

If the philosophical implications of Buddhism and the ideal of nonself or nonexistence seem discouraging to the Western mind, the ethical implications, as taught by Gautama, are both positive and noteworthy. The negation of self eliminated selfishness, and Gautama stressed love and service to others. With time, the striving for personal salvation by one's own efforts (Hinayana Buddhism) was displaced in many regions by reliance on the help of a savior (Mahayana Buddhism), and effort on behalf of all mankind rather than of oneself or one's country became the ideal.

Gautama shared the Hindu view of the worthlessness and painfulness of physical craving, but he opposed the ascetic extreme of self-torture no less than worldly overindulgence. As unconcerned as the Hindus about the formulation of a dogmatic body of doctrine which all believers must accept, Gautama supplemented religious openmindedness with the concept of equality; all men, regardless of worldly status, were equally able to become Buddhas ("Enlightened Ones"). At odds with the caste system, his was a native heritage of values, on which modern ideals of political and social democracy can draw for support. But though Buddhism was to prevail in the spiritual realm of most of the Far East, it failed to establish itself permanently in the land of its origin. Though it flourished under King Asoka, its patron, it undermined the military strength of his dynasty, and generally militated against the formation of a strong nation state.

Islam, introduced by the Turkish and Afghan invaders of the eighth century A.D., was a "revealed" religion, imbued with the dogmatism of the Judaeo-Christian tradition, from which it had drawn freely. It was highly militant; its followers believed that death incurred in the propagation of the faith to the far corners of the world was a sure and speedy road to paradise. But though it spurred on the Moslems in their conquest of the subcontinent, it too failed to provide a rallying point for unification. The intolerance and cruelty of the Moslem forces aroused popular hostility and only exacerbated internal disunity.

The Portuguese arrived in India during the so-called Delhi Sultanate, the declining years of Turko-Afghan rule. For the first century and a half of their sway, the fierce Moslems had given the subcontinent a strong government, but in the second half of the fourteenth century they had fallen prey to internal disunity and the devastating onslaught of the central Asian forces of Amir Timur (Tamerlane), whose ghastly cruelty had earned them the sobriquet "Earth Shakers." An attempted resurrection of the Delhi Sultanate in the fifteenth century had succeeded in name more than in fact, and when the Portuguese arrived, the Turko-Afghan rulers did not have control of the old regions of the Sultanate. Over a dozen Moslem and Hindu states vied for power. The internal religious antagonism and political division and strife, which rent the subcontinent apart, facilitated, if it did not invite, foreign encroachment. Not only did the rival states fail to make common cause against the Portuguese, but by threatening each other they even prevented effective local resistance.

The numerous invaders had been drawn to India by its natural wealth. The monsoonal climate of the largely tropical subcontinent nourished an agrarian economy of rice, cotton, jute, and spices, especially in the Indo-Gangetic plain — the heartland of Indian civilization and, to this day, the main seat of her population. In size, as in variety, this population has always been remarkable. As early as the fifth century B.C., the Greek historian Herodotus characterized the Indians as "more numerous than any other nation with which we are acquainted," and today the population of India approaches one-fifth of all mankind. During the latter years of the Delhi Sultanate, notwithstanding the political and religious turmoil, the labor of India's teeming millions combined with the natural wealth of the subcontinent to support thriving ports, where native and foreign merchants exchanged local products and wares from Southeast Asia, the Near East, and Europe.

Satisfied at first to purchase such treasures as the spices of the East Indies through the Persians and the Arabs, the Europeans (from Venice, Genoa, and even Russia) pushed to India in the fifteenth century in an attempt to eliminate the middleman. The successful and highly profitable negotiation of the round-trip crossing, by sea around Africa, of Vasco da Gama from Lisbon to Calicut (on the western coast of India) in the late 1490's, opened the way for direct relations between western Europe and India and the lands to the east.

The Portuguese, who were in the forefront of European maritime explorations, retained a monopoly of European dealings with India until the seventeenth century, and Lisbon became the hub of a flourishing trade. Their great fleets of ships plied the Indian Ocean; da Gama's expedition of 1501, for example, consisted of twenty vessels. The Portuguese mariners drove the Arabs from the sea both by economic competition and by force, as religious hatred joined arms with commercial advantage. In the second decade of the sixteenth century the Portuguese took possession of Goa, Malacca, Bombay, and other Indian ports, establishing commercial bases and military garrisons reinforced by native troops. Well received by the Indians when they first arrived, the Portuguese by their aggression and their religious persecution of Moslems and Hindus soon aroused popular hostility, thus contributing to the Indian legacy of anti-Westernism.

The establishment of the Mogul dynasty in northern India in the sixteenth century by Babur and his Moslem, mostly Mongol, followers confronted the Portuguese with a strong, relatively

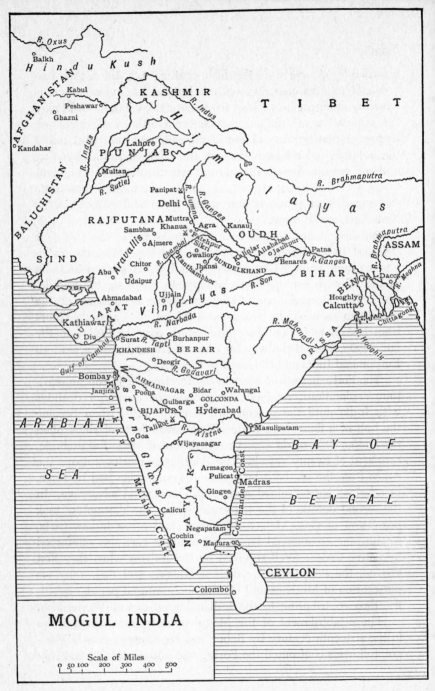

MOGUL INDIA

Scale of Miles

0   50 100   200   300   400   500

From W. H. Moreland and Atul Chandra Chatterjee, *A Short History of India;* copyright, 1953, Longmans, Green & Co. Limited.

united state, and halted (though it did not roll back) Portuguese encroachment. It was Babur's grandson Akbar the Great,
who, as mentioned already, did most to provide the foundations
for Indian unity. A man of ambition and iron will, of great
physical strength, an ardent sportsman, endowed with a sharp
mind and a good memory, alert, curious, hard-working, and with
a gift for selecting competent advisers and officials, Akbar was
the equal in stature of his illustrious contemporaries Elizabeth I
of England and Philip II of Spain. Like them, he extended the
authority of the central government. The administrative system
which he evolved outlived the Mogul dynasty, continuing into
British times. Through his prime minister, his revenue minister,
his viceroys who headed the provinces, through governors and
judges — in short, through an extensive and highly organized
salaried civil service — he exerted effective authority. So well
were the finances of his state organized that on his death he was
reputed to have been the richest of all contemporary rulers.

Unlike Philip II, who was noted for his bigotry and tried
to unify Spain through religious conformity, Akbar saw the
strength of his dynasty in tolerance, and wooed the support of
men of all faiths. From the Portuguese, with whom he remained on relatively good terms, he desired not merely European firearms; he invited Jesuit fathers to his court and conversed
with them repeatedly. A Moslem by background, Akbar turned
his back on his original beliefs and developed an eclectic religion, designed to accommodate the views of all. He treated
Hindus with more consideration than Moslems, usually removing
defeated Moslem rulers and extending direct central administration to their territory, while leaving Hindu rulers, who
pledged loyalty, in actual control of their lands. In earlier years
of Moslem rule the attitude had been, "If the tax collector chooses
to spit into the mouth of a Hindu, the latter must open his
mouth without hesitation." Akbar discontinued this sort of arrogant oppression, and extended civil as well as religious tolerance to Hindus. He banned the slave raids, which had victimized
many Hindus, and interdicted the consumption of foods to
which native religions objected. By tolerance and justice he

succeeded in broadening the political support of the Mogul dynasty, a support which it generally retained until later Mogul rulers departed from Akbar's principles and once again alienated the Hindu majority.

In the first quarter of the seventeenth century the Dutch and English East India Companies established trading posts (so-called factories) and forts at various points along the Indian coast — at Surat, Masulipatam, Pulicat, and Armagon. Their motivation was commercial, the Dutch being particularly attracted by the fact that in India, unlike the East Indies islands, their desire for cotton goods and spices was reciprocated by native demands for silver. The Portuguese, of course, detested competition, Protestant competition at that, but their forces in India, as in Southeast Asia, were no match for Dutch naval power, and they were driven eventually from everywhere save Goa. Moreover, the Moguls saw in trade with the Dutch and English more than economic benefits; it permitted them to strengthen their own position by playing the foreigners off against each other. The Indians had still no naval force of their own, and were vulnerable to Western pressure, but though disputes and incidents were not lacking, the Europeans were as yet concerned primarily with the smooth flow of commerce. Since conflict was bad for the mutually profitable business, a relatively amicable *modus vivendi* therefore prevailed between Indians and Westerners throughout most of the seventeenth century.

The foreign trade augmented the knowledge Indians and Europeans had of each other's products, countries, and ways of life; it did not, however, entail any cultural exchanges at this time. The literary culture of the Mogul court was mainly Persian, though Akbar and his successors collected also translations of Sanskrit writings. The Mogul style of art, which flowered in the seventeenth century, was a blending of the native talents and traditions of Indian artists and the Persian manner which they sought to follow. Under Shah Jahan (1628–58), grandson of Akbar, the splendor of Mogul architecture and applied arts reached its peak; Europeans were awed by the opulence of Mogul rule. The highly ornate, bejeweled Taj Mahal, erected by

Shah Jahan at Agra as a marble mausoleum for his wife and himself, remains one of the architectural wonders of the world.

The cost of such courtly luxury was borne by the people, and Shah Jahan's overtaxation of the peasantry shook the economic stability of his dynasty. Oppression was especially heavy in the south, where Mogul supremacy had come to be recognized. When Aurangzeb (1659–1707), son and successor of Shah Jahan, aggravated the economic plight of the populace by severe economic and religious persecution of the Hindu majority, the foundations of the Mogul dynasty were completely undermined. Rebellion and unrest, banditry and piracy prompted the English and the Dutch and the French (who had established a factory at Surat in 1668) to fortify their positions, and native traders and craftsmen moved to Madras, Bombay, and Calcutta, within the security of British protection. By the middle of the eighteenth century the Mogul empire had fallen apart.

The "free-for-all" contest, in which Hindu, Moslem, and other contenders strove to outmaneuver and overcome each other, enabled the Europeans to manipulate Indians against Indians, and Hindus against Moslems, just as the Indians had once played foreigners against each other. The wanton cruelty wreaked by the various conquering armies of the native states, notably the Maratha confederacy, drove ever more Indians into regions protected by European firearms, which wrought havoc among the native cavalry. The Persian capture and looting of Delhi in 1741 gave added emphasis to the impotence of the Mogul regime. Conditions were ripe for the evolution of European leaseholds into colonial possessions.

During the European War of the Austrian Succession, the French and English forces, swelled by European-officered Indian infantrymen, called "sepoys," clashed in India (1746–48). Following the termination of hostilities, both sides were faced with the cost of maintaining inactive troops and solved the problem by lending them out to contending factions on the Indian scene. This precipitated, however, a renewal of French and English armed conflict, which was to become coextensive with the Seven Years' War in Europe. Though at first (about

1751) it seemed that the French were on the way to dominance, the British emerged victorious, and by 1760 were left to hold the field. The way was clear for the English East India Company, under the able governorship of Robert Clive and his successors, Warren Hastings and Lord Cornwallis, to embark on the gradual conquest of the subcontinent.

CHINA

The sea route to China, as to India, was discovered by the Portuguese, but Western relations with China, as with India, were of more ancient origins.

Unlike India, China did not "wait" to be discovered. In the second century B.C. the Chinese envoy Chang Ch'ien set out for the west in search of the Scythians (Ta Yüeh Chi), whom Emperor Wu of the Han dynasty hoped to enlist as allies against their common enemy, the Huns (Hsiung Nu). After much hardship, including ten years of Hun captivity, Chang got as far as Bactria in Central Asia; and though he failed to induce the Scythians, with whom he at last caught up, to re-enter the fray, the accounts he brought back encouraged Chinese penetration into Sinkiang. At the dawn of the Christian era (in 2 A.D.), Chinese vessels may have crossed the Indian Ocean for the precious stones, pearls, and rare animals obtained in exchange for gold and silk. In the last decades of the first century (between 73 and 102 A.D.) Pan Chao, in renewed quest for allies against the Huns, led a large army to the Caspian Sea, while one of his officers actually pushed on to the Persian Gulf, so that only the Caspian Sea and the Armenian mountains stood between the empires of Rome and of Han China. No direct contacts were made, but trade resulted, and Chinese products, especially silk, drained gold from the Roman empire. Western motifs found their way into Chinese art, and generally more information reached China about Rome than reached Rome about China.

The economic and political collapse of the Roman empire, political strife within China, control of the land and sea routes between China and Europe by hostile peoples, and the development of sericulture and hence the production of raw silk in the Byzantine empire conspired to interrupt Chinese dealings with the West, yet in the seventh century A.D. the Chinese were once again near the Caspian Sea. Now Byzantine embassies appear to have traveled to China, partly in search of allies against the Moslem Arabs; and Persians, Greeks, Indians, Arabs, and other foreigners flocked to Ch'ang-an, the magnificent capital of the T'ang dynasty. With them they brought Western ideas — Nestorian Christianity, Manichaeism, Zoroastrianism, Islam, and Judaism. Foreign trade was notable no less for its thorough organization than for its prosperity, and many regulations and concepts of modern times (extraterritoriality, for example) have roots in the T'ang period. But with the collapse of the Roman and T'ang empires and the loss of control of the routes between them to nomadic peoples on land and to the Arabs on the sea, relations between China and the West were again suspended; and in the four centuries of separation which followed, the knowledge that Europe and China had of each other all but faded away.

Mongol conquests and the imposition of the Pax Mongolica over most of Eurasia did more than merely restore safe lines of communication in the thirteenth century. The Mongols built highways which expedited travel between China, Persia, and Russia, and employed Europeans and Central Asians in China, and Chinese in Europe and the Near East. During the Mongol sway Marco Polo visited China and, though it had suffered greatly under Mongol occupation, brought back a starry-eyed account of its prosperity and might. The possibility of using the Mongol empire as a confederate against the Turks suggested itself to the Christian West, and as other Europeans flocked to China they were more observant of local conditions than had been the merchants of Greek and Roman times. Roman Catholicism was brought into China; gunpowder, printing, porcelain, playing cards, and other Chinese inventions were carried westward. The break-up of the Mongol empire disrupted overland travel. But the Chinese of the Ming dynasty in the first half of the fifteenth century thrust south and westward in a series of mighty naval expeditions to the East Indies, India, Arabia, and Africa. On the eve of the Portuguese explorations, the Chinese controlled the Indian Ocean and had power enough to have withstood European encroachment. But they withdrew into their continental shell of their own volition as court interest in the expeditions waned. The seas were open to the Europeans.

The China which the Portuguese "discovered," about 1514, resembled India in that it was huge in territory — roughly the size of all of Europe — heavily populated, and ancient in history and tradition. Like India, it had a fluvial civilization, centering in the fertile valleys of great rivers. Like India, though situated farther north and generally less tropical in climate, China was subject to the rain-bearing monsoon winds that blew against or along its arching coastline. Indeed, no factor was more significant in the shaping of Chinese civilization than the monsoonal division of the Chinese land mass into two distinct regions — the brownish, water-starved, loess-covered north, and the green, rain-soaked south — and the corollary development of a system of large-scale water works for irrigation and flood control.

Like India, too, China was not a nation in the modern sense. Like "India," "China" and "Cathay" were foreign appellations; the former was derived from the dynasty of the first empire (Ch'in), and the latter, like its Russian equivalent "Kitai," from the name of a people in the north (the Khitans). The Chinese themselves spoke of "Under Heaven" and "Within the Four Seas" and "the Central Kingdom," and thought of themselves as "the Men of Han" and "the Men of T'ang" or, more generically, as "the

black-haired people." As in India, civilization had begun in the
north (in the valley of the Yellow river) and had gradually
spread southward (to the Yangtze valley and below). As in
India, different peoples had been involved — Mongols, Tunguese,
Turks, Tibetans, and Thai. As in India, there were different
religions and different spoken languages. But here the similarity
ends. Despite repeated political division and foreign occupation, despite differences in race, language, and religion, China
was held together by a common culture, more uniform and per-
vasive than the Hindu way of life.

Of the many schools of thought which had competed for the
minds of the Chinese in the Classical Age (roughly between the
eighth and third centuries B.C.), Legalism and Confucianism
had emerged victorious. Legalism recognized neither religious
nor moral values. The material strength of the state was its sole
objective, in pursuit of which it encouraged agriculture and war.
The bases of a strong rule, it believed, were harsh laws and the
skillful meting out of rewards and punishments. Confucianism
was more humane. It upheld virtue and rule by moral example.
Confucius (551–479 B.C.), its founder, was a realist who felt
that "the measure of man is man." Aware that fruitful teaching
begins with the cultivation of the teacher's own character, he
taught what might be called applied ethics. The most important
work handing down his sayings, the *Analects*, compiled by his
disciples decades after his death, contains but fragments of his
thought, at the heart of which were virtue, benevolence, and
good will between men. The Confucian canon in later years
came to consist of the so-called Five Classics and Four Books,
the latter until recent years prescribed for study in all elementary
schools. Among the most interesting of the Four Books, were
the *Works of Mencius*. Mencius (372–289 B.C.) taught that man
is good by nature, that political and economic systems exist for
the welfare of the people, and that the ruler must strive to improve the living conditions of his subjects. Unlike the *Analects*,
which sound in parts like a collection of slogans, the *Works of
Mencius* are fascinating stories, expounding the psychology of
ethics and good government. But in spite of religious overtones

in later centuries, Confucianism, like Legalism, was essentially concerned with human relations, with this world.

The spiritual needs of the Chinese people were filled by Taoism and Buddhism. Taoism, the religion of "the Way," was a noble, serenely philosophical school of thought. Like other Chinese schools of thought it concerned itself with the governing of the people. But it regarded the state, indeed civilization, as the source of suffering and unrest. The Taoists were political, intellectual, and moral anarchists. The Taoist classic, the *Tao-te-ching,* one of the world's greatest religious works, exhorted man to adjust to nature, not interfere with it. With popularization, Taoism degenerated into alchemy and superstition, into a magic quest for happiness, wealth, and eternal life. But the lessons of the *Tao-te-ching* — the wisdom of appearing foolish, the strength of weakness, and winning by yielding — have become an important part of the psychological make-up of all Chinese. Buddhism was introduced from India in its later and less demanding Mahayana form. Generally speaking, Taoism and Buddhism were confined to the populace at large. The educated elite, from which the officialdom was selected by examination, turned its back on mystical contemplation. Further, since Taoism and Buddhism were tolerantly open to outside influences, and Confucianism was the official philosophy, Confucian precepts filtered into both, and ethical considerations made inroads on metaphysical speculation. Questions of government became the major concern of philosophers. In this, China and India were at opposite poles. Indeed, they had less in common with each other than each had with contemporary Europe, for the Christian outlook on life fell about midway between the other-worldly extreme of Indian thought and the this-worldly extreme of Chinese tradition.

The examination system, based on a knowledge of the Confucian classics, provided a common body of knowledge and values for officials and would-be-officials throughout China, and perpetuated a common orthodox tradition over the centuries. It joined China together geographically and chronologically in a cultural bond which weathered every political storm and for-

eign occupation until modern times. The Confucian task was
facilitated by the peculiarity of the Chinese written language.
Unlike the words of Indo-European tongues, which remained
meaningless until mentally pronounced, Chinese characters were
pictorial and symbolic representations, basically independent of
sound. One character, for example, would be a stylized picture
of the sun; another a picture of the moon. Joined together, the
two pictograms would form a third character, an ideogram,
conveying the meaning "bright." The sun rising behind a tree
would indicate "east," and so forth. The characters represented
absolute ideas; words were not inflected; there was no distinction
between nouns, verbs, or adjectives, nor between case or tense,
the function of each word being gleaned from context. While
the spoken language evolved into dialects as different as the
diverse tongues in Europe, the written language, independent of
sound, remained quite constant from the third century B.C. on,
and, like the arms of the Confucian examination system, extended
Chinese culture to all regions and all times.

There was a universality to the Chinese language, which was
characteristic of the whole Confucian outlook. The state was not
a national concept; it was all that the appellation "Under
Heaven" conveyed. As a part of the universe, whose natural
order was reflected in its governmental structure, the state was
headed by an emperor, the "Son of Heaven," who performed,
on behalf of all, the rites due to Heaven. From Heaven he had
a mandate to rule, a mandate which Heaven withdrew in the
event of unvirtuous conduct. Natural calamities were regarded
as the expression of Heaven's displeasure, and the people had the
right to rebel against the ruler who had forfeited the mandate.
Thus dynasty followed dynasty, and the mandate passed from
hand to hand. In theory, as there was but one sun in the sky,
there could be but one ruler on earth, and the tendency developed on the part of the people, when the mandate began to
slip, to go over to the winning rival, to whom the Mandate of
Heaven had evidently been transferred. A reflection of the
universe, the state was at the same time an extension of the
family, social and political relationships being overshadowed

both in theory and in fact by family relationships. The role of the emperor was that of the stern but benevolent father; the duty of the subjects, that of filial sons. The head of the family performed religious rites for his family. It was as the head of all families, as the father of fathers, that the emperor performed the rites to Heaven. Ancestor worship, as the ministration to the needs of the spirits of departed ancestors is misleadingly called, was the ultimate expression of filial piety and loyalty to the family and, by extension, to the emperor.

The Confucian emphasis was on propriety, decorum, and harmony. Like Buddhism, Confucianism advocated moderation; unlike Buddhism, which believed that everyone, regardless of social status, could aspire to Buddhahood, it insisted that everyone and everything be in the proper place. With all its class-consciousness, however, Confucianism did not by "proper place" envisage anything akin to the Hindu caste divisions. Anyone willing to conform to Chinese customs was treated like a Chinese. Society was stratified into four layers: scholars, farmers, artisans, and merchants. But the upper stratum comprising the scholars was open, in theory at least, to anyone who passed the appropriate examinations, and "proper place" had a far less rigid and finite meaning in China than in India. Soldiers were not included in the social scale. From the Confucian point of view, as one did not use good metal to make a nail, so one did not use a good man to make a soldier.

Confucianism, it must be remembered, was a product of the Chinese scene, where the large-scale water works, so necessary to the Chinese economy, were beyond the means of individuals. It is therefore not surprising that Confucianism allocated to the government an active role in the economic, social, and educational development of the country. The officials through whom the government acted were rotated from province to province, and though the intent was essentially to prevent any official from acquiring undue local influence, this rotation contributed to the dissemination of a common culture.

History was regarded as a mirror for government, and, unlike the Indians, whose interests were other-worldly, the Confucianists compiled lengthy official historical accounts, which furnished a ready framework for the study and perpetuation of Chinese civilization. To the Confucianists, as to the modern Communists, history was also a tool for moralization and indoctrination, and traditional accounts of China's origins painted an idyllic centralized empire which provided Confucian theoreticians with alleged historical precedents for their ideas. Actually, the authority of the kings of the first historical dynasty, the Shang, in the second millennium B.C., was confined essentially to religious matters. The rulers of the Chou, who overran the Shang domains from the west in the eleventh century B.C., administered a larger region through a network of military garrisons commanded by relatives and allies. (Neither the Chou, nor the Shang before them, were Chinese, in the historical definition of the term. It was the blending of Shang, Chou, and native elements that gave birth to Chinese civilization.) By the eighth century B.C. the power of the Chou kings had waned, and the thousand-odd feudal states which surrounded the Chou heartland retained but the loosest connection with it. Thus China first truly entered the ken of history not as an idyllic centralized state but as a feudal realm, which in time became the scene of uncontrolled intrigue and open warfare between rival states.

If the Chou period in political structure outwardly resembles Europe's Middle Ages, culturally it compares with the Classical Age of the Greek city states. Numerous schools of thought — Confucianism, Legalism, Taoism, Moism, Yin-Yangism and many others — were developed at this time by philosophers, who could peddle their intellectual wares, pregnant with political advice, at the contending feudal courts. The price of unification in later years was to be political and intellectual orthodoxy, but the influence of the Classical Age in China remained more lasting than that of the Classical Age in the West. Unlike Europe, where Christianity transformed the ancient tradition into a new civilization, China, notwithstanding the contributions of Buddhism, preserved the Confucian (and Taoist) heritage of Chou times without drastic modification.

In 221 B.C. the state of Ch'in emerged supreme in the struggle for China, and the country was unified by Shih Huang Ti, the "First Emperor." Unification was not merely military. With the aid of his able minister Li Ssu, Shih Huang Ti created a genuine central administration with an elaborate bureaucracy. The written language, weights and measures, and the gauges of wagons were standardized. Wide, tree-lined roads were constructed. Irrigation projects were begun, and agriculture was stimulated. Harsh laws were universally applied. Subversive (non-Legalist) literature was burned and criticism of the government was forbidden. The position of the emperor was boosted to a level of mystery and unapproachability. The frontiers of the empire were extended, and secured with Chinese colonists. Internal feudal fortifications and walls were demolished. At the same time, the separate walls in the north were joined into one Great Wall, clearly separating China from the nomadic world beyond. By these measures Shih Huang Ti laid the basis for the unification of China. But the burden on the populace was heavy, and Shih Huang Ti's dream that his family would rule for ten thousand generations barely outlived his own death. It was the Han dynasty which carried Shih Huang Ti's plans to fruition, mellowing his Legalist measures with Confucian doctrine. So intertwined were the aims and reigns of the Ch'in and the Han, that the label "First Empire" is usually applied to them jointly.

The Han dynasty, with but a brief interruption in the early years of the first century A.D., ruled China from about 202 B.C. until 220 A.D. It saw a great advance in culture, large-scale expeditions (including the ones to the West, mentioned earlier), imperialistic expansion, and the development of the Confucian state system, which, with relatively minor changes, continued until modern times. Eventually the luxury of court life and the machinations of eunuchs, concubines, and others at court undermined the vigor of the Han dynasty, and provincial generals, one after another, began to assert their power. The First Empire fell apart into rival kingdoms.

Three and a half centuries passed before China was reunified by the Sui and T'ang dynasties. The long interlude of dis-

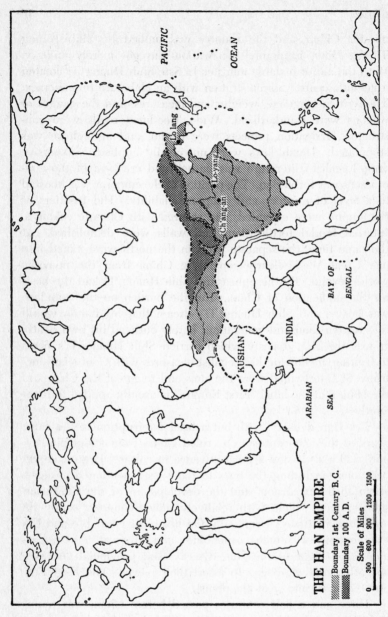

THE HAN EMPIRE

Boundary 1st Century B.C.
Boundary 100 A.D.

Scale of Miles
0   300   600   900   1200 1500

PACIFIC

OCEAN

Lo lang

Lo-yang

Ch'ang-an

BAY OF

BENGAL

INDIA

KUSHAN

ARABIAN

SEA

From L. Carrington Goodrich, *A Short History of the Chinese People*; copyright, 1943, Harper & Brothers.

union, during which northern China repeatedly fell victim to foreign invasion, resembled the Dark Ages of European history, but its impact was less devastating, and Chinese civilization retained a greater cultural continuity than Western civilization. Buddhism, which had been introduced from India during the Han period, flourished in the years of anarchy. With reunification, Confucianism reasserted its dominance. But not at once. Yang Chien, who founded the Sui dynasty in the sixth century A.D., had imbibed the militarism and rank-consciousness of the nomadic tribes against whom his state (Northern Chou) had fought. From his officials he desired soldierly obedience, not scholarly rationalization. His son and successor Yang Ti, however, patronized Confucianism again. Where his father had aroused resentment by excessive economy, Yang Ti precipitated the collapse of his dynasty by extravagance. Many of the measures, such as the joining of the Yellow and Yangtze rivers by a canal, were vital to China's long-term development, but their immediate cost was high, and the Sui dynasty, like the Ch'in, did not last long enough to enjoy the fruits of its labors. The T'ang, which followed the Sui in 618 A.D., like the Han which had succeeded the Ch'in, reaped the harvest its predecessor had sown at the cost of its life.

In the three centuries of T'ang rule, China attained a new pinnacle of power and prosperity. It seems to have been the largest and most populous empire of the time. Territorial acquisitions were matched by commercial expansion, and, as noted already, the harbors of China were thronged with foreign merchants. Wood block printing was invented, and Confucian, Buddhist, and Taoist texts disseminated, the earliest extant printed book being a copy of the Diamond Sutra (one of the Mahayana scriptures), printed almost six hundred years before the Gutenberg Bible.

The disunity which followed the collapse of T'ang rule in the tenth century was less threatening than the interlude after the Han. By now the ideas of unity and a centralized Confucian state were firmly implanted in the hearts and minds of the Chinese. Yet the Sung dynasty (founded in 960 A.D.), which may be regarded as the third centralized empire, failed to re-unite the whole of China, the northern regions remaining under the domination of successive groups of nomadic peoples — the Khitans, the Jurchens, the Mongols, and others. China's forced separation from the overland trade routes, however, fostered a thriving overseas commerce and Chinese domination of the Indian Ocean. Steeped in an atmosphere of peaceful prosperity, with diplomacy rather than arms its primary means of defense, the Sung plunged into cultural pursuits, especially painting, with unequaled enthusiasm.

The reunification of China was the work of foreigners — the Mongols, who overran the country toward the end of the thirteenth century. The Mongol sway (the Yüan dynasty, 1280–1368) is an important landmark in Chinese history. Though not without some benefits — the security of travel between east and west, for example — it was generally so severe and humiliating as to arouse in the Chinese a nationalistic hatred of foreigners and an intense longing for the "good old days." The eventual withdrawal of the Mongols was due more to their own weakness and their desire to return to the lands of their fathers than to Chinese military might. Nevertheless, China's liberation left the Chinese with a superiority complex which, joining hands with the dislike of foreigners and the longing for days gone by, inhibited subsequent Chinese history by overemphasis on the ways and values of the past.

Under the Ming dynasty (1368–1644), during which the Portuguese arrived, China was well governed and prosperous. Once again China was united under native rule, and Chinese authority was extended to upper Burma and Annam. Great maritime expeditions, such as the world had never before known, in the first half of the fifteenth century visited the East Indies, the Indo-Chinese peninsula, Ceylon, India, Persia, Arabia, and Africa — all this while the Portuguese were still feeling their way down the west coast of Africa. The expeditions, however, having no solid economic or political basis, were discontinued because of official dissatisfaction with their costliness and jealousy of their captaincy by a eunuch (Cheng Ho), and China reverted

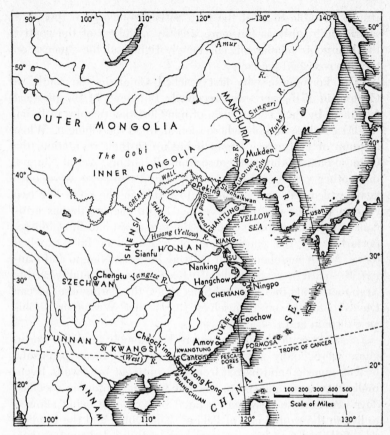

MING CHINA

From G. N. Steiger, *A History of the Far East,* Ginn and Company, Boston, 1936.

to the ancient prohibition against travel overseas. This inward orientation was in the spirit of the times. Throughout the greater part of the Ming period China faced backward, its accomplishments dulled by imitation, conformity, and mediocrity. The one advance — the slight democratization of the predominantly landed oligarchy of scholars by the addition of scholars from the budding bourgeoisie — had disappointing results. Unable to meet the high costs of office from their low salaries as readily as the more wealthy members of the gentry, the bourgeois scholar officials merely tightened the squeeze on the impoverished peasantry.

The Portuguese who first reached China in the south, at Canton, in 1516, were well received. But news of the piratical treatment by their countrymen of non-Christian peoples in India, the East Indies, and elsewhere soon alarmed the Chinese. When a group of Portuguese began living up to their reputation, the Chinese banned the Portuguese from all harbors. Yet at Ningpo, in another province to the north, the Portuguese were once again welcomed, and permitted to reside in the city. For two years a prosperous trade developed, until the murderous arrogance of the Portuguese came to the fore again and the Chinese, perturbed by the construction of a European fort, expelled them. At Ch'üan-chou, about halfway between Ningpo and Canton, the pattern repeated itself. Received as hospitably as the Arab merchants in T'ang and Sung times, the Portuguese "Ocean Devils" brought on themselves (and other Westerners) Chinese disdain and restrictions.

Yet trade could be made to pay handsomely, and the Portuguese were finally permitted to stay on the Macao peninsula, heavily guarded and barred from the continent by a wall. Eventually they were allowed to trade at nearby Canton on specified days. Portuguese missionaries fared better, some being allowed to live in the capital city of Peking. The Dutch and the English, who followed to China as they had to India, behaved as barbarously as the Portuguese. Their robbing and murdering of Chinese merchants in the East Indies and the Philippines was well known in China, and it is likely that all these Europeans would have been expelled from China, had not the Ming dynasty, as it went under in its struggle with the Manchus, clutched at the straw of foreign aid. The Jesuit fathers proved valuable instructors in mathematics, astronomy, and gunnery, and a Portuguese fighting force was actually recruited by the Ming. Though this force never saw the field of battle, the close association of the Jesuits with the Ming court made the Portuguese doubly suspect in the eyes of the Manchus when they came to power in the seventeenth century, and the old restrictions on trade were continued. But the scientific, military, and diplomatic services of the Catholic fathers, who were suffered to remain in Peking, prompted the relaxation of trade limitations. In the second quarter of the eighteenth century, however, the outbreak of a heated controversy between different Catholic orders over the proper translation of the word "God" into Chinese, and over the question of permitting Chinese converts to continue the traditional ancestral rites, finally led, after papal intervention, to the expulsion of the missionaries, while English and Dutch trespasses and the persistent fear of European support for southern rebels resulted in the renewed confinement of European contacts (excluding overland relations with the Russians) to Canton.

The Manchus, who ruled China from 1644 until 1912, were themselves foreigners, hailing from Manchuria. They discriminated against the Chinese in government employment, and forced them, as a sign of submission, to wear the Manchu dress and hair-do — the long queue. But they hired Chinese scholars and themselves adopted Confucian ways so thoroughly that by the twentieth century, underneath their Manchu garments, they had become Chinese in culture.

During the first century and a half, Manchu rule was vigorous. China proper was pacified; the peripheral areas of Manchuria, Mongolia, Sinkiang, Tibet, and Taiwan (Formosa) were brought directly into the realm of the Manchu Ch'ing dynasty; and the Liu Ch'iu (Ryukyu) islands, Korea, Nepal, Burma, Laos, Siam, and Annam were made into tributaries. Not only did the Manchu empire excel all previous Chinese empires (not counting Mongol rule) in territory, but in prosperity and population too it reached a new high. The introduction by the Europeans of such supplementary food crops as the sweet potato helped boost the Chinese population from about 63,500,000 in the sixteenth century to over 275,000,000 by the end of the eighteenth century, making the Manchu empire the most populous empire in the contemporary world. As late as the eighteenth century,

before the Industrial Revolution and the humanitarian movement in the West, China was at least as advanced as Europe
in material prosperity and in justice and humaneness of administration. The great Manchu monarchs K'ang Hsi (reigned
1661–1722) and Ch'ien Lung (reigned 1736–96) were more
than the equals of their illustrious European contemporaries
Louis XIV, Peter the Great, William III, Catherine the Great,
and Frederick the Great. Not without reason did Ch'ien Lung,
in 1793, turn down a British request for trade with these words
to the mad king of England, George III:

> Swaying the wide world, I have but one aim in view, namely, to
> maintain a perfect governance and to fulfill the duties of the State.
> Strange and costly objects do not interest me. If I have commanded
> that the tribute offerings sent by you, O King, are to be accepted,
> this was solely in consideration for the spirit which prompted you
> to despatch them from afar. Our Dynasty's majestic virtue has
> penetrated into every country under Heaven, and kings of all na-
> tions have offered their costly tribute by land and sea. As your
> Ambassador can see for himself, we possess all things. I set no
> value on objects strange or ingenious, and have no use for your
> country's manufactures.[1]

The Industrial Revolution was to change the power relationship between China and Europe. It was to be the tragedy of
China that the Manchu dynasty, cut off intellectually from Europe
after the expulsion of the missionaries, would be unable to com-
prehend the significance of the transformation of Europe and
to make the necessary adjustments.

[1] Arnold J. Toynbee, *A Study of History* (London: Oxford University
Press, 1939), I, 161.

SOUTHEAST ASIA

The Portuguese had made their way to India to eliminate the middleman in the spice trade. When they learned, upon reaching India, that most of the spices actually came from still farther east, the Portuguese pushed on. In 1509 they reached the port of Malacca, on the southwestern shore of the Malay peninsula, and, after a successful conflict with its Arab masters in 1511, made it the center of a prosperous commercial empire, establishing commercial relations with the neighboring regions.

Commanding by its geographic position the most direct approaches from India and lands west to the Far East, the Malay peninsula had been the object of repeated contention. Arab traders had frequented the East Indian archipelago since early in the Christian era, and Malacca had been the seat of Arab power and the leading harbor in Southeast Asia in the fourteenth and fifteenth centuries. Originally subjected to Indian and Chinese influences — the Malays, the dominant racial group, had come from southern China — the cultural heritage of the

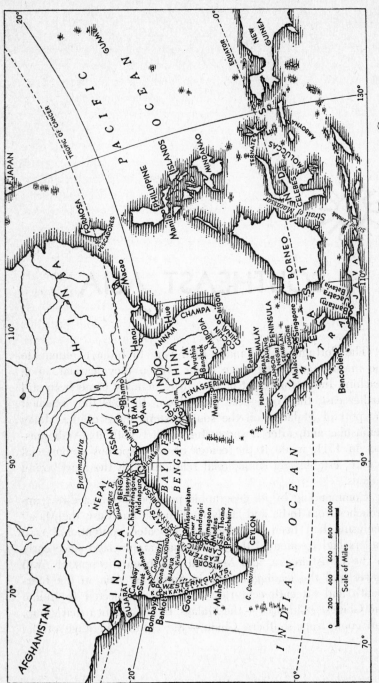

SOUTHERN ASIA AND THE EAST INDIES IN THE SEVENTEENTH AND EIGHTEENTH CENTURIES

From G. N. Steiger, *A History of the Far East*, Ginn and Company, Boston, 1936.

Malay peninsula in the sixteenth century was partly Hindu, partly Buddhist, partly Moslem. The spoken language was of the Malayo-Polynesian family, with Arabic as the written script.

Reaching toward the equator, the Malay peninsula was an extension of the Indo-Chinese peninsula. Wedged between India and China, the Indo-Chinese peninsula, with its different races and religions, had a culture which was to a great extent an amalgam of Indian religious and artistic elements and Chinese political and scientific concepts. Indian influence was strongest along the west coast of the Indo-Chinese peninsula and its Malayan extension, for Indian merchants had come across the Bay of Bengal. Chinese influence, on the other hand, was rooted most firmly in the northeastern half of the peninsula, the region known in modern times as Annam. Readily accessible by land, Annam had been directly subject to Chinese political influence, for it had recognized the authority of the Chinese emperor in the third century B.C., and from the second century B.C. to the tenth century A.D. had been under Chinese rule. It is not surprising that Chinese concepts persisted in this region even in the five centuries of native administration which followed.

To the south of Annam, on the Indo-Chinese peninsula, lay Champa. Beyond the military reach of the Chinese, it had been under Indian rule in the second century A.D., and had been Hinduized within the next half century. Yet its geographical location had induced it to play an intermediary role in the commerce of Arabs, Persians, and Indians with China, and, overawed by the civilization and might of the Sung and T'ang dynasties, it had repeatedly, from the seventh century on, paid tribute to the Chinese court.

Cambodia, south of Champa, also showed Indian and to a less extent Chinese influence. From the late ninth century A.D. until its defeat by the Siamese in the thirteenth, Cambodia, ruled by the Khmer, had been the dominant power of the Indo-Chinese peninsula. Visited by the Europeans in the sixteenth, seventeenth, and eighteenth centuries, it was to lean on French assistance and thereby leave itself open to later French domination.

Siam (Thailand), Burma, and Tibet, to which the Portuguese and other Europeans also penetrated in the Age of Exploration, were equally mixed in population make-up and similarly indebted to Indian and Chinese culture. As elsewhere in Southeast Asia, the Chinese influence was most evident in the political sphere, the Indian influence in religion and art.

More important, from the point of view of relations with the West, than these relatively inaccessible regions, were the numerous islands just across the Malacca Strait, the East Indies, with their colorful array of inhabitants of Malay, Mongoloid, Negroid, Papuan, and other extraction, who in most areas, like the people of the Malay peninsula, had received the greater part of their civilization from India, and some from China, and had ultimately grafted Islam to their Buddhist and Hindu heritage. Because of their strategic location, the East Indies, especially the islands of Sumatra and Java, had since pre-Christian times been the centers of Indian and Arab commercial empires. When the Europeans arrived — first the Portuguese, then the Dutch, and later (temporarily) the English — they found no strong Indian, Arabian, Chinese, or native dynasties, and they made these islands the nucleus of their spice trade. But Christianity, in spite of concerted missionary effort, made little headway against Islam, and the impact of European rule was generally less notable for the changes it made in the life of the islanders than for the effect it had on the economic development of the European powers.

Like the East Indies, of which they were a part geographically and racially, the Philippine islands too had imbibed Indian, Chinese, and Moslem influences. Unlike the East Indies or the Indo-Chinese peninsula, however, the Philippines were profoundly changed by their exposure to Western rule. Conquered not by the Portuguese or the Dutch, whose primary concern was commercial, but by the Spaniards in a series of expeditions from Spain proper and from Mexico in the sixteenth century, the Philippines were Europeanized more thoroughly than any other Asian region. Though of limited commercial value to the Spaniards, the Philippines formed an important strategic base in the Pacific.

Taken as a whole, the lands of tropical Southeast Asia were vast in extent — about half the area of the present-day United States — and rich in spices and other products coveted by the Europeans of the Age of Exploration. They had a common heritage of Indian, Chinese, and, in places, Moslem influence. But the peoples of the East Indies did not think of themselves as Southeast Asians. There was no racial, national, linguistic, or social unity in the region as a whole any more than in the various kingdoms of which it was composed. Even more diversified than India, and weaker, Southeast Asia offered fertile ground for European encroachment.

JAPAN

East of the Asian coast, and arching out from it like a bow, lies the chain of mountainous islands known as Japan. News of Japan first reached Europe in the thirteenth century through Marco Polo, who during his service at the Mongol court in China learned of the unsuccessful Mongol attempts to invade these islands. In the early sixteenth century the Portuguese, active in the South China Sea, may have encountered Japanese seamen, but real contacts between Europeans and Japanese did not take place until about 1542, when three Portuguese on a Chinese junk, en route from Siam to Ch'üan-chou, were driven by a typhoon to a little island south of Kyushu. The hospitable reception of the Portuguese beckoned on their countrymen, and before long a wave of Portuguese traders and priests broke over the islands.

The Japan which the Portuguese thus discovered, quite by accident, was very different from India or China. It was an island empire, whose mixed population had immigrated from the Asian continent, and also, perhaps, from the South Sea islands. Whereas fertile river valleys nourished the civilizations of India and China, a mountainous terrain severely limited the cultivable area of the Japanese archipelago and pushed the hardy inhabitants onto the sea in quest of food. Compared with China and India, the three main islands (Kyushu, Shikoku, and Honshu — Hokkaido had not yet been colonized) were infinitesimal in size and young in history, though compared with Europe they were larger in area than the British Isles and of respectable antiquity. More distant from the mainland than England, Japan was close enough to continental Asia for repeated transfusions of people and ideas, yet at the same time far enough to develop a distinct civilization of its own. The Japanese home, with its sliding doors, straw mats, picture alcoves, and bath, is a persisting reminder of the strong native roots of Japanese culture.

According to Japanese tradition, the Japanese empire was founded in 660 B.C. by Emperor Jimmu, a descendant of the Sun Goddess. Its nucleus was the region of Yamato, near the eastern reaches of the Inland Sea, and the name "Yamato" is occasionally applied by extension to all Japan. The empire in early times seems to have been governed by numerous clans, of which the imperial clan was the most powerful. The faith of ancient Japan was Shinto. Commonly but misleadingly translated as "the Way of the Gods," Shinto was a polytheistic veneration of nature and supermen, "shin" (or, to give this Chinese-derived term its Japanese reading, "kami") signifying anything superior. It was a primitive religion without a moral concept of sin; "sin" was merely ritual impurity, whether produced by murder or childbirth. Only after the introduction of Buddhism and Confucianism into Japan, in about the sixth century A.D., did Shinto develop the moral aspects and political mythology of later years. It was the function (and source of authority) of the clan chieftains to worship the clan deities, beseeching their succor in such matters as good crops. The introduction of Buddhism, which ignored the clan deities, and of Chinese learning, which advanced irrigation ditches, reservoirs, and the calendar as more reliable sources of agricultural success, undermined the political position of the clan chieftains and facilitated the establishment of a centralized imperial government after the Chinese pattern in the seventh century.

Still borrowing freely, the Japanese tried to copy the institutions of the great T'ang empire. The establishment of the first "permanent" capital at Nara in 710 A.D. culminated the period of unashamed imitation, in which everything Chinese set the standard. Gradually the Japanese became more selective, and adoption evolved into adaptation. During the Heian period (794–1167) Chinese influence was thoroughly Japanized.

The Heian period, so named after the new capital of Peace and Tranquility (Heian-kyo) at Kyoto, was Japan's Classical Age. Without a written language of their own, the Japanese had adopted the Chinese characters, which, as we have seen, were pictorial and symbolic representations, basically independent of sound. At first, writing was left to immigrant scribes, who continued to write in pure Chinese. Gradually attempts were made to use some of the characters for their sound and to record the Japanese language phonetically. Out of these attempts there was developed during the Heian period a Japanese syllabary, now numbering forty-eight symbols, simplified evolutions of Chinese characters, conveying the sound of whole syllables: *a, i, u, e, o; ka, ki, ku, ke, ko; sa, shi, su, se, so;* and so forth. In this syllabary, the court ladies of the Heian era wrote Japan's greatest literature, notably *The Tale of Genji*, a lengthy novel by Lady Murasaki Shikibu. The men, engrossed in Chinese studies and disdainful of the simplicity of the syllabary, continued to write in Chinese. The use of Chinese characters alone to write Japanese proved impractical, for the latter language, in contrast to Chinese, was inflected. It is a good example of the eclecticism of the Japanese, that they eventually adapted the pictorial characters of monosyllabic Chinese to the words of polysyllabic Japanese by the addition of the phonetic syllabary, so that the written Japanese language of today is essentially a conglomeration of Chinese and Japanese.

The Tale of Genji, written early in the eleventh century, vividly depicted the remarkable sophistication and effete luxuriousness of the imperial court, which set the tone of Heian culture. Poetry and song, stylish dress and flowers in bloom, Buddhist ritual, the pursuit of butterflies, and a melancholy awareness of the impermanence of everything prevaded Heian life. There was neither the Indian preoccupation with metaphysics nor the Chinese interest in human relations. Not the ascetic nor the ethic, but the aesthetic dominated Japanese thought, and the appreciation of beauty emerged as one of the most characteristic traits of the Japanese tradition.

During most of the ninth, tenth, and eleventh centuries Japan was ruled by the writing brush. Civil administrators dominated the scene. Key positions were held by members of the Fujiwara family, which had jockeyed itself into pre-eminence by supplying the imperial line with consorts. As relatives of the emperors, the Fujiwara encroached ever more on imperial authority, until they became the power behind the throne, the *de facto* rulers of Japan. Fujiwara dominance reached its height in the closing years of the tenth and the first quarter of the eleventh centuries, when the great Fujiwara Michinaga, father-in-law of four emperors and grandfather of four, held the reins of government as regent for thirty years. So secure was his position, so resplendent his court, that he could boast, "the moon changes every month, but I remain the full moon always."

Yet in the luxury of Fujiwara rule there lay the seeds of the civil bureaucracy's destruction. Engrossed in the civilized life at court, the Fujiwara officials were reluctant to venture into the crude countryside, and neglected its administration. When conditions in the distant regions deteriorated, and dissatisfaction ignited rebellion, the Fujiwara did not have the power to cope with the situation themselves, but leaned on military clans outside the capital. Emperors who had grown weary of Fujiwara domination sought to shake it off by retiring, and ruling as retired emperors from temples, free of Fujiwara influence. The rivalry between the courts of the reigning and retired emperors, the military demonstrations of some wealthy Buddhist monasteries, and dissension among members of the large Fujiwara family itself, strengthened the hand of the outlying clans. Called upon to do the fighting now of one faction, now of another, the military themselves eventually emerged as supreme, and the struggle for control of the government became translated into a conflict between two military clans — the Taira and the Minamoto.

For eighteen years (1167–85) the Taira had the upper hand, but in the final quarter of the twelfth century the Minamoto emerged victorious. Leaving the emperors to head a sham government at Kyoto, Minamoto Yoritomo moved the effective seat of government to Kamakura in the east and there received imperial appointment as Shogun or Generalissimo (an abbreviation of Sei-i Tai-Shogun, Barbarian-Subduing-Generalissimo). From then until 1868 Japan was ruled by hereditary military dictatorships. Called "shogunates" in English, they were known in Japanese as "bakufu" or "tent governments." Relatively stern, frugal, and soldierly, they instilled into the Japanese tradition the standards and virtues of the military. Although they usurped the imperial authority, the shoguns did not abolish the imperial sovereignty or enthrone themselves. The emperors in Kyoto, shorn though they were of practically all but religious and ceremonial functions, remained the legal sovereigns of Japan.

Shogun Minamoto Yoritomo was a man of strong character. When his sons were unable to fill his place, power slipped into the hands of his remarkable widow, Masako. Thus the military dictators, who had usurped from the emperors actual control of the government, themselves became puppets, and Masako and her Hojo relatives in Kamakura played a role similar to that of the Fujiwara in Kyoto. Clan loyalty, military virtues, and behind-the-scenes rule remained characteristics of Japanese government until modern times.

It was during the Hojo sway that the Mongols attempted to conquer Japan. Twice, in 1274 and 1281, they launched gigantic amphibious invasions from Korea. Both times they were forced to withdraw to their vessels, both times the vessels were sunk or scattered by typhoons. To the Japanese, who had always claimed divine extraction, the typhoon ("big wind") appeared as a "kamikaze" ("divine wind"). The isolation of Japan, the experience of the Mongol invasions, and the belief in spe-

cial divine protection contributed to the rise in Japan of a nationalistic spirit, not found elsewhere in the world beyond
Europe until the twentieth century. But the Hojo, whose administration of the country had for many years been as efficient
as their defense efforts had been valiant, had no spoils of victory with which to repay their followers for their contribution in
the long struggle with the Mongols. Dissatisfaction mounted, and
when the degeneration of Hojo rule invited rebellion, another
military family, the Ashikaga, seized the reins of government
in the 1330's. The Ashikaga shoguns, who ruled from Kyoto, did
not have the power of the early Minamoto or Hojo, however.
In spite of a prosperous trade with China in the late fourteenth
century and repeated cultural bloom then and later, Japan had
cracked open politically by the beginning of the fifteenth century. In 1336 the reigning emperor had fled from Ashikaga
dominance; and as the Ashikaga named a replacement, two
rival houses — the northern and southern dynasties — complicated
the political situation. A compromise to let the two lines rule
alternately created new problems, and when disputes over the
succession erupted within the Ashikaga family, the whole country drifted into disorder. From the second half of the fifteenth
century till the third quarter of the sixteenth, Japan was torn
by civil war.

The military dictators lost their grip; the emperors were
powerless and destitute. Local chiefs vied with each other for
supremacy, while famines and epidemics decimated the population. When by the seventeenth century Japan was unified again
through the genius of three military men — Oda Nobunaga, Toyotomi Hideyoshi, and Tokugawa Ieyasu — the layers of Japanese society gave the appearance of having been turned over
with a gigantic plow. The old aristocracy had all but sunk out
of sight, while men of low birth and high ability had been thrust
to the surface. Untrammeled by tradition, the unifiers were
receptive to new ideas and methods, if only these promised
success. Yet they were warriors, and once again, and more
effectively than ever, Japan was ruled by a military central government. So ardent was the martial spirit of Toyotomi Hideyoshi,

who completed the military unification begun by Oda, that
it was not confined by the borders of Japan, but in the 1590's
spilled over to the Asian continent, to Korea, in a bid for the
mastery of the Far East.

Tokugawa Ieyasu, who emerged as top man upon the death
of Toyotomi, moved the seat of government back to the east,
to the new city of Edo, the Tokyo or "Eastern Capital" of today.
The emperor continued as legal sovereign in the ancient capital
of Kyoto, but actual power rested in the hands of the Tokugawa
shogunate. The Tokugawa family with its various branches and
immediate vassals owned between a quarter and a fifth of the
country's agricultural land and derived its revenue therefrom.
The remainder of the land was in the hands of warrior-lords,
who, though they exercised a considerable degree of local autonomy, were vassals of the shogun, and their followers, the samurai
or warrior-knights of Japan. Politically, the Tokugawa structure spelled centralized feudalism. Socially and economically,
Japan was stratified into four classes of population: warriors,
farmers, artisans, and merchants. The ruling elite, amounting
with its families to about one-sixteenth of the population, was
a hereditary class of fighters, forbidden to pursue any other
vocation.

Tokugawa Japan was a police state par excellence. The domains of the feudal lords were so reshuffled as to place the most
reliable vassals in strategic positions throughout the country, one
guarding against another. The imperial court was isolated
so that no feudal lords could approach the emperor except with
the permission of the shogun. The shogunate itself was isolated, above the reaches of the people. And most important
of all, the feudal lords were partially isolated from their own
domains and families. By the ingenious system of "alternate
residence" every lord and vassal of importance had to spend a
stipulated period of time in the new capital, maintaining there
a residence corresponding to his position. The expense of maintaining such a residence the year round, not to mention the trip
to the capital and back with a suitable retinue, diminished the
economic power of the feudal lord. At the same time his periodic

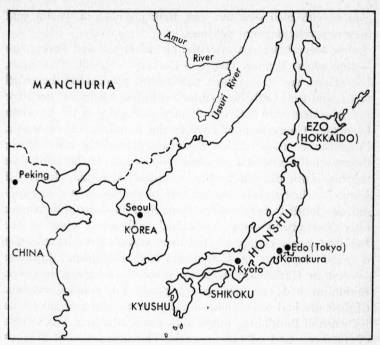

JAPAN AND THE MAINLAND IN THE AGE OF EXPLORATION

absences weakened his hold on his own domain. And when he returned to his territories, his family had to remain in the capital as hostages. Carefully enveloping Japan in a net of government control and discouraging initiative and unconformity by the severity of its punishments, the Tokugawa system succeeded in perpetuating itself for over two and a half centuries.

But when the Portuguese arrived, Japan was still waist-deep in the morass of civil war; the country had not yet been reunified. Even after reunification in the early years of the seventeenth century, her leaders were still insecure and suspicious, guarding against conspiracy from any quarter. They did not repel the Christians outright, however. Despite the ravages of civil war Japan had retained her intellectual alertness. The foreigners with their new weapons, their promises of wealth, and their new religion were welcome.

For several decades after the arrival of the first Portuguese — throughout Japan's "Christian Century" — Jesuit, Franciscan, Dominican, and Augustinian missionaries propagated the "tried and tested true Catholic doctrine" with less hindrance from the Japanese than from their own limited knowledge of the Japanese language. Converts numbered in the hundreds of thousands. Buddhism envisaged a lengthy chain of rebirths after death; the new faith promised paradise upon death. At the same time the new faith did not appear excessively different. Indeed it seemed at first merely another sect of Buddhism, for not only did the Jesuit fathers pattern themselves in dress and manner after Zen priests — the intellectual and social elite of the Buddhist clergy in Japan — but there was a resemblance in the outward trappings of Catholicism and Buddhism. Japanese interest in Christianity was not primarily religious, however. Buddhism had been introduced partly for political reasons. Christianity had some political utility as a counterweight to the influence of Buddhism. But mainly it was attractive as a vehicle of commerce and military strength. This association of firearms and other Western products with Christianity was both the strength and the weakness of the Church. It facilitated the introduction of Christianity into Japan, yet resulted also in its expulsion.

Christianity was not confined to the poor and weak. When Japanese forces overran Korea, Christian officers and troops formed one of the spearheads. These officers, as well as Christian leaders elsewhere, were a potential menace to the Japanese polity. By its very nature Christianity was politically subversive, infringing on the demands of the totalitarian state. Nor did the missionaries simply withhold from Caesar what was not Caesar's; they encroached on Caesar's domain and sought to guide the political consciences of their flock. Increasingly the resemblance between Christianity and Buddhism faded. Confident of their foothold in Japan, the fathers unveiled the less seemly attributes of seventeenth-century Catholicism: fanatical intolerance, the Inquisition, conversion by the sword, and political intrigue.

The Japanese were disappointed in the returns of foreign trade and feared lest the potentially hostile feudal lords on the outskirts of the empire unduly strengthen their power by the acquisition of Western firearms. They were aware of the political machinations of the fathers and listened with interest to the advice of English and Dutch Protestants who eagerly reported how their kings dealt with Papists. They were shocked by the flagrant European traffic in Japanese slaves, who in poverty-stricken Japan cost so little that even the Negro and Malay servants of the Portuguese speculated in them. They were disgusted with the endless murderous brawls among the low foreign adventurers who resorted at the Japanese seaports — murderous brawls which cast suspicion on the sincerity of Christian professions. In the interest of political and social stability, the leaders of Japan felt that the rising tide of Christianity and foreign influence must be turned back.

On July 25, 1587, Toyotomi Hideyoshi ordered the missionaries to leave Japan within twenty days. But they did not respect his commands, and went on with their preaching. When the Japanese would bodily place them on a ship and deport them, they would merely return in disguise. In exasperation the Japanese resorted to stronger measures, first against the native converts, then against the foreign missionaries. The threat of torture and execution did not deter the fathers, however. With renewed determination, indeed with hope and spiritual longing, they chose the path to martyrdom.

Anti-Christian in expression, the drive to eliminate foreign thought and influence extended eventually to merchants as well, and led to a series of decrees which all but terminated Japan's intercourse with the West. The last and most comprehensive of these was the edict of June, 1636, which prohibited the departure of any Japanese vessel for a foreign country and forbade on pain of death any Japanese to go abroad or, if abroad, to return. It provided for the deportation of any foreign offspring and its foster parents. It called for the continued ferreting out of Christian missionaries and native converts, and offered two hundred to three hundred pieces of silver for information leading to the discovery of a Jesuit, while threatening with arrest any foreigner who aided the priests.

In 1623 the English had left Japan of their own volition. The following year the Spaniards were expelled. Now with the edict of 1636 the door of Japan was almost closed. Then in 1637 a serious rebellion of Japanese Christians broke out, and the Portuguese seemed implicated. In 1638 they too were expelled. The door was shut. Yet there was a barred cell-like window through which glimpses of the world could be espied. This window was Deshima, a fan-shaped little island, artifically constructed off Nagasaki in 1641, on which the Dutch, who had followed to Japan in the 1580's, were suffered to retain a precarious foothold throughout the period of seclusion. Shrewd traders that they were, the Dutch had deflected the wrath of their inquisitors to their Catholic competitors, had hidden, if not denied, their own Christianity, and had proffered their services to the Japanese with humility.

The Japanese saw the advantage of a window upon Europe through which they could receive whatever foreign goods they might desire and, more important, through which they could keep abreast of European designs. Every year the Dutch had to submit a report about the latest world happenings. Yet for all their usefulness, the Dutch were treated without honor or respect, indeed at times like the most dangerous of criminals. Deshima measured only 82 common paces in width and 236 in main length, yet it contained a number of buildings in which the Dutch lived: wooden two-storied cottages, the lower floors of which were used for storage of goods; special fireproof warehouses; a kitchen; and buildings for the transaction of sales, for the accommodation of gubernatorial deputies, for fire apparatus, laundry, Japanese guards, interpreters, and so forth. When Dutch ships paid their annual visit to the harbor and their crews hung about on Deshima for two or three months, the island seemed to be bulging at the seams, but upon their departure only the factor and several companions remained to keep a lonely vigil.

They were completely isolated from Japan. A high, roof-covered, deal-board fence topped by a double row of pikes hemmed in the island, while large posts erected in the water clearly marked the line beyond which no Japanese must trespass. The two strong gates which faced the water on the north were never opened except when Dutch ships were laden or unladen under strict supervision. A small stone bridge joined the island with Nagasaki, but on the city side there was a guardhouse and normally the end of the road. Even the fire holes for fetching water were nailed shut, and the gutters which ran into the sea had purposely been made crooked to forestall any communication with the outside.

The unification and seclusion of Japan ushered in a period of prolonged peace. For the sake of internal order the martial spirit of the samurai had to be restrained, and the ruling class of Japan became increasingly parasitic — forbidden to work, forbidden to fight. To make matters worse, the economic and ideological foundations of the Tokugawa system were unsound. The power of the shogunate and its vassals was based on an economy of agriculture. Rice was the measure of wealth, the means of payment for the services of the samurai. But the institution of "alternate residence," though it indisputably provided political protection, so stimulated commerce as to foster the development of a money economy and the concomitant rise to influence of merchants and financiers, as well as the growth of an essentially anti-feudal urban culture in the capital itself, which by the eighteenth century had become the largest city in the world. Meanwhile the shogunate's attempt to deflect the energies of the warriors from military to intellectual pursuits stimulated the study of Japanese history and the ultimate realization that the shogun was a usurper of imperial prerogatives. The efforts of foreigners to reopen Japan were to meet with increasing receptiveness as more and more Japanese became dissatisfied with the conditions of the day and began to consider foreign trade and foreign methods as a possible means of rejuvenating Japan.

Among the various schools of learning that flourished in

Tokugawa Japan, the most interesting in this connection was the "Rangaku" or "School of Dutch Learning," which eventually included under the same name English, French, and Russian studies. With the prohibition of Christianity a ban had been imposed not only on Christian literature but on all Western knowledge. As the fear of European subversion gradually subsided, this ban was modified to apply to religious writings only. After 1720, Japanese scholars were able to devote themselves to the study of Dutch language, medicine, natural science, mathematics, astronomy, and military science. The restrictions on the Dutch were relaxed enough to permit them to assist the Japanese scholars in such endeavors. Japan had closed her door, but Deshima served as window through which the Japanese could peer at the world outside.

Epilogue: Part One

The world beyond Europe, which Western explorers, merchants, and missionaries discovered in the sixteenth, seventeenth, and eighteenth centuries, was the home of different races, religions, civilizations, and social structures. In India, for example, the priesthood constituted the ruling elite; in China, the civilian scholars; in Japan, the military. Acquaintance with the different customs and values of the non-Western world played a part in undermining European faith in the perfection of Christian institutions. The leading figures of the Enlightenment read with avid interest the glowing reports of the Jesuit scholars in Peking. The stability and grandiose framework of the Confucian bureaucracy, the competitive civil service examinations, the stress on human relations and rational moral science, the development of secular ethics and social philosophy evoked the admiration of such men as Leibnitz, Voltaire, and Quesnay. The Deists found support for their outlook; the Physiocrats found a fertile source for some of their doctrines and plans. In short, in the days of the Enlightenment the organization of the Chinese empire appeared (as Voltaire put it) "in truth the best that the world has ever seen." Chinese influence also pervaded European fashions. The architecture of Chinese pavilions and pagodas, Chinese silks, porcelain, and lacquer, "Chinese-Gothic" Chippendale furniture, and paintings of chinoiseries went hand in hand with the Rococo style. Chinese-English gardens delighted European eyes, while China tea and the spices of India and Southeast Asia titillated European palates. No such strong influence was exerted by the West on the world beyond Europe at this time.

Different as the civilizations of Asia were from each other, they had one feature in common: in the Age of Exploration they compared favorably with the civilization of Europe. They were economically self-sufficient and relatively powerful. This was especially true of China, not only of whose justice and administration but of whose roads, bridges, and water works the Europeans wrote with admiration. To be sure, when the Portuguese first arrived in the Far East, India, China, and Japan were in a state of internal weakness and division, but before the Europeans were able to come in large numbers, India, China, and Japan saw the rise to power of new ruling families, which, in China and Japan at least, succeeded in holding the foreigners at bay.

In the Middle Ages, India, China, and Japan had outshone Europe. It was in the Age of Exploration that Europe burst its frontiers and throughout the world gained footholds which were later to become springboards for conquest. The attempt of China and Japan to avoid foreign entanglement by restraining their own expansion in Southeast Asia left the field to the Westerners. The commercial profits, which the Europeans were to reap undisturbed in consequence, were to provide the wherewithal for the Industrial Revolution and usher in a new chapter in world history.

B.C.	NEAR EAST AND EUROPE			INDIA
2000				
1900				
1800	Egyptian epoch			
1700				
1600				Indo-Aryan invasions
1500				
1400				
1300				
1200				
1100				
1000				
900				
800				
700	Greek epoch			Epic period
600				
500				
400				Early Hindu period
300				
200				Maurya empire
100				
A.D.				
100	Roman epoch			Nomadic invasions
200				
300				
400				Gupta empire
500				
600	The Middle Ages	Byzantine empire	Moslem civilization	
700				
800				
900				
1000				Renewed invasions
1100				
1200				
1300				
1400				
1500				
1600	Modern Europe			Mogul empire
1700				

EPOCHS
of Exploration

CHINA	JAPAN	B. C
		2000
Hsia dynasty		1900
		1800
		1700
		1600
		1500
Shang dynasty		1400
		1300
		1200
		1100
		1000
	Clan period	900
		800
Chou dynasty		700
		600
		500
		400
		300
		200
		100
		A. D.
Ch'in-Han empire		100
		200
		300
Political disunion		400
		500
	Centralization of government	600
Sui-T'ang empire		700
	Nara period	800
Political disunion		900
	Heian period	1000
Sung dynasty		1100
Mongol (Yüan) empire	Military dictatorships: Taira, Minamoto, Ashikaga	1200
		1300
		1400
Ming dynasty	Country at war	1500
		1600
The Manchu (Ch'ing) empire	Reunification: Tokugawa shogunate	1700

PART TWO

IN THE AGE OF IMPERIALISM

INDIA

The Age of Imperialism found the British firmly entrenched in India. The English government had not planned the subjugation of India; not until 1813 did it actually extend British sovereignty to the acquisitions of the East India Company on the subcontinent. It was the English East India Company that effected the spread of British power, more in spite of government interference than because of government support. Indeed, the company itself had not consciously set out on a policy of territorial expansion; it had begun in trade but it ended in empire.

The East India Company was a joint-stock trading company, chartered by the Crown in 1600, and privately owned. Like any corporation, it was run by a board of directors, who appointed governors and other officers to carry on company affairs in India. Successive royal renewals of its charter enlarged the sphere of its activities and empowered it to exercise civil, criminal, and military jurisdiction on a princely scale. By 1788 Edmund Burke could aptly say that "in fact the East India Company in India is a State in the disguise of a merchant." During its first

century and a half the company operated primarily as a trading
venture, but amid the turmoil that followed the collapse of
Mogul rule, and as an outpost of the Anglo-French struggle, it
became involved in Indian politics and conflict, where ascen-
dency and victory generally meant the acquisition of new territory. With Parliament's passage of the Regulating Act (1773)
and the India Act (1784), the sovereignty and administration
of the territories in India began to pass from the company to the
Crown-in-Parliament, in an unplanned, evolutionary process that
was not completed until 1858. Thus there is a grain of truth in
the often quoted assertion that Great Britain conquered India
in a fit of absentmindedness. Absentminded or not, by the 1840's
the British controlled the entire subcontinent, either directly or
through protectorates.

British rule was not without benefit to the Indian peoples.
Cruel customs, such as widow-burning (suttee), ritual strangu-
lation, and infanticide, were eliminated. New concepts, such as
government of law, parliamentary institutions, and democratic
rights, were introduced. Interest in science was developed, both
as the means of industrialization and as the vehicle for secular
thought. Modern roads and harbors were built, and the country
was connected by postal and telegraph services, railways, and a
national system of education. The use of English in administration and education was of particular importance, for India
was thus at last provided with a common means of communication. In short, the foundations for a modern Indian nation
state were laid by the British.

Many of the English administrators kept in mind the eventual
self-government of India. The period from 1828 to 1856, under
the governor-generalship of Lord William Bentinck and then of
Lord Dalhousie, was especially constructive, even liberal. But
unlike earlier conquerors of the subcontinent, the English kept
themselves almost completely apart from the natives socially,
depriving themselves of the opportunity to keep abreast of Indian thought and feelings. The violence of the Sepoy Mutiny,
which was triggered in 1857 by the distribution of cartridges
sacrilegiously greased with animal fat, shattered the hope that

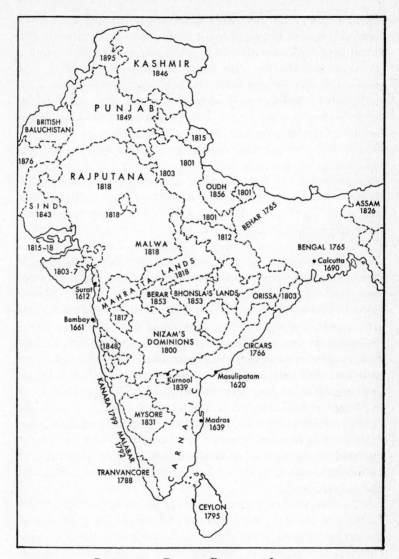

GROWTH OF BRITISH POWER IN INDIA

After William L. Langer, *An Encyclopedia of World History;* copyright, 1952, Houghton Mifflin Company.

Western ways could peaceably transform India. The East India Company was at last abolished (1858); the British government, which now took over the direct administration of the colonies, chose not to interfere with native customs and religions, and concentrated on keeping things as they were.

British control was secured by the Indian army, officered by Englishmen and manned primarily by traditional Indian soldiers — Sikhs, Gurkhas, Punjabi Moslems, and Pathans — and by alliances with the partially dependent princely states. The administration of the subcontinent, headed by the Secretary of State for India and the Council of India in London, and by the governor-general (viceroy) and an executive council in India, was in the hands of the Indian Civil Service, whose senior positions were staffed with Englishmen of generally remarkable ability and dedication. With pride in their White Man's Burden these administrators did give India during the Pax Britannica a greater degree of peace, law, order, famine relief, personal freedom, local representation, and political unity than she had ever enjoyed. Yet in all their efficiency and honesty, the British administrators lost sight of any long-range goal. They excluded Indians from senior positions in the civil service, and in their daily routine became themselves increasingly divorced from the populace. Not only were Indians given unequal political status, in being excluded from determining policy for their own country; they were also treated as inferior in every other respect, socially, morally, culturally. No doubt various local customs were reprehensible from an objective modern point of view, but the repeated singling out of these shortcomings by missionaries and reformers to underline the importance of their own work created a distorted image.

Reforms affected various elements in Indian society differently. For example, the unification of the Indian market and the organization of trade with Europe permitted the fuller distribution and exportation of grain. This decreased the oversupply in some regions, raising the price (to the delight of the producer and the disgust of the consumer) and bringing good profit to the commercial middleman. Hygenic improvements, the prohibition of infanticide, measures to prevent famine, and the establishment of civil order were all to the public good, yet they created as many problems as they solved, for the population soared from about 100,000,000 in the seventeenth century to almost 300,000,000 by the beginning of the twentieth. Industrially, British dominance had dislocated much of the native economy, causing severe distress among the masses. At the same time, however, the increased commercialization of the country had brought to the fore a small but influential bourgeoisie — merchants, bankers, and professional men. Members of this class frequently received a British education. Exposed to Western liberal thought, they became doubly resentful of the inferior status accorded to them in their own country. Their intellects were awakened to nationalism by their study of European history; their hearts were filled with nationalistic ardor as a result of humiliation at the hands of the white man.

Generally speaking, the British allowed India a free press and did not silence vocal criticism. A considerable latitude of political expression was thus given to India's newly trained journalists, teachers, and lawyers, from among whom many of the nationalist leaders came. Such men as G. K. Gokhale and Surendranath Banerjea organized associations which clamored for political and social reforms. Not essentially anti-British, though they strove for ultimate self-government, these native leaders and the Indian National Congress, in which they met from 1885 to debate vital issues, received considerable support from private Englishmen. Gokhale and Banerjea were great admirers of the West, and Indian nationalism in its early stages derived much inspiration from European history. But in the last quarter of the nineteenth century Indian nationalism assumed a more native character. The men of the Hindu Renaissance, as the revived interest in the Indian past is often called, did not share the earlier nationalists' hope of rejuvenating India with Western ideas; they rejected Western culture as materialistic. Marshaling their ancient religious beliefs in support of modern nationalism, they attributed divinity to Mother India. These Hindu nationalists, notably Dayananda Saraswati and

Vivekananda, directed their attacks not only against the West, but also against their Moslem countrymen. To be sure, in traditional Hindu fashion, they regarded no religion as false; still, Hinduism, they asserted, was the "Mother of Religion." This attitude alarmed the Moslems in India, who, in their efforts to rejuvenate their strength through Western learning, kept fairly well apart from the Hindus. In the 1890's Hindu nationalism, under the leadership of Bal Gangadhar Tilak, reached a militant height, religiously defending everything Hindu and opposing all alien religions and ways uncompromisingly and with violence.

Conditions in India were favorable to the nationalist cause. In the 1890's natural calamities — famines, plagues, monsoons, and droughts — claimed the lives of hundreds of millions of people, leaving the British with a staggering relief problem and a discontented colonial population. The failure of Lord Curzon, the English viceroy, to appreciate the intensity and extent of Indian nationalism added fuel to the smoldering fire. When with the best of intentions he increased government control over Indian universities in order to raise academic standards (1904), he aroused Indian intellectuals as one man; when, following this, he partitioned the great province of Bengal to improve the efficiency of local administration (1905), he unleashed a wave of protest that expressed itself in vast public demonstrations. Increasingly the Indians were beginning to assert themselves, politically, culturally, and in every other respect. It was becoming clear that British rule in India, sooner or later, would have to come to grips or to terms with the rising spirit of nationalism.

SOUTHEAST ASIA

By the middle of the seventeenth century the Dutch had gained control over most of the East Indies. The Dutch East India Company ruled the islands with varying degrees of directness. In some regions the native chieftains were prevailed upon to grant to the company trading privileges in return for military assistance; on Java, on the other hand, the native chieftains were reduced to the position of outright vassals, required to pay a stipulated annual tribute.

Interested exclusively in protecting its profits, the company resisted proposals made by the colonists for free trade and for the colonization of some of the islands. In the interest of economy and with regard solely for the collection of tribute, it left local administration in the hands of oppressive native chieftains. In the long run this policy proved unsuccessful, and widespread smuggling, graft, and mismanagement brought ruin to the company by the end of the eighteenth century. In 1798, amid the colonial repercussions of the French Revolutionary and Napoleonic wars, the company's life ended, and control of its territories passed to the French-controlled Netherlands, thence for half a decade to British rule, and finally, by the peace treaties following the Napoleonic wars, to the Kingdom of the Netherlands. The assumption of control over the East Indies by the Dutch government brought little relief to the natives. Forced to cultivate coffee, sugar, and indigo for the markets of Europe, they frequently had to neglect the food crops needed for their own subsistence.

With the spread of liberal ideas in Europe and the adoption of a new constitution in the Netherlands in 1848, however, the Estates-General in response to public pressure began to ameliorate conditions in the colonies. This public pressure was not native but Dutch; the subject peoples, except for some Moslems in northwestern Sumatra, offered little opposition to Netherlandic domination. The reforms extended to the Dutch colonies in the second half of the nineteenth century included the revamping of the civil service, the development of public education, and the abolition of forced labor and forced production. These reforms brought beneficial results not only to the islanders themselves but to the whole Dutch economy, as the colonies became a growing market for European goods. The standard of living of the native population did not increase proportionately, however, since prosperity was expressed primarily in a rising birth rate.

Burma fell prey to British imperialism. An Anglo-Burmese rivalry developed over Assam, which lay between the kingdom of Burma and the Indian province of Bengal, where the British had established themselves. This rivalry, fanned by conflicting commercial interests, broke out in repeated warfare until in the third quarter of the nineteenth century the British annexed the kingdom, promising to the Manchu government, whose vassal Burma had been, that Burmese missions would continue to visit Peking with local products.

During the Napoleonic wars the British had acquired control of the East Indies. Though they restored the greater part to the Dutch after the Congress of Vienna, they retained the southern extremity of the Malay peninsula, including the island and magnificent port of Singapore (obtained by purchase from the Sultan of Jahore) as well as Malacca (obtained from the Dutch in exchange for another post on Sumatra). Extending their domination northward, the British formed the Straits Settlements of Singapore, Malacca, and Penang into a crown colony (1867), and to the north, a number of sultanates into the Federated Malay States (1896).

Annam, like Burma, found opposition to Western interests futile. While the British were occupied with the Sepoy Mutiny in India (1857), the assassination of a French missionary in Annam gave Napoleon III the pretext to use force, and by the following year his troops secured Cochin China, with the excellent seaport of Saigon. From here the French extended their influence to Cambodia, which Siam, the former suzerain, forewent without a struggle to escape inroads on her own territory, and obtained from Annam additional territory adjacent to Cochin China. In the late 1870's and early 1880's the French turned the whole of Annam into a protectorate after crossing swords with Manchu China, its suzerain. In 1893 and in the early years of the twentieth century France further extended her Indo-Chinese possessions at the expense of Siam. The first years of French rule were marked by corruption, mismanagement, and native rebellion. By the end of the nineteenth century, however, the introduction of much-needed reforms improved local conditions and thereby strengthened French rule.

The Dutch, English, and French competed also for influence and commercial profit in Siam, but Siam deftly walked the tightrope of independence. Her success was due in part to her geographical position between the British and French possessions, for the rival powers wished to preserve a buffer state between their territories. It was due also to the stability and enlightenment of her ruling dynasty, notably the reigns of Rama IV (1851–1868) and Rama V (1868–1910), whose ready conclusion of commercial treaties with the Western powers, adoption of a modern educational system and of Western commercial and legal methods, and general modernization of the country deprived the imperialistic powers of the usual opportunities for aggression.

The United States, whose early commercial interest in East Asia had been deflected first by her own civil war, and then by the reconstruction period and the development of the American frontier, resumed a more active role in the closing years of the nineteenth century. In 1898 Hawaii was annexed. In the same year, on defeating Spain, the United States took over the Philippine Islands and thereby became a colonial power with a vested interest in developments in the Far East and Southeast Asia. The United States inaugurated sweeping reforms in the Philippines, and after overcoming the armed resistance of Filipinos who wanted independence, transferred the administration of the islands from military to civilian hands, with increasing native participation.

CHINA

The pressure of the West on China has come from two main directions: from the north by land and from the southeast by sea. The Russians, whose seventeenth-century push across the enormous Asian continent to the Pacific shores (and beyond to America) is too often overlooked by students of the Age of Exploration, were the first Europeans to conclude a treaty with China, the Treaty of Nerchinsk in 1689. Signed one hundred and fifty-three years before the first treaty of Great Britain with China, it was negotiated on the part of the Russians from a position of weakness, for the Manchu forces exceeded anything the Russians could muster in the Far East at the time. Like the Treaty of Kiakhta (1727), which supplemented it, it was of necessity an "equal" treaty, Russia obtaining no excessive concessions from China. These treaties delineated the Russo-Chinese frontier (the longest contiguous frontier in the world), provided for regular commercial relations overland, and even permitted the establishment of a Russian Orthodox mission in the Chinese capital at a time when Westerners were generally barred from the interior. Yet the mission was not a center of propaganda. It catered to the spiritual needs of Russians and served as a window upon China. No doubt the prolonged contact provided Russians with that special understanding of the Chinese which many observers have attributed to a common Asian heritage. Russian ability to deal with the Chinese had its political applications, as we shall see, but in general the impact of Russia on China in the Age of Imperialism differed in character from the impact of Great Britain and the United States. It was almost exclusively commercial and military (as had been the impact of earlier invaders from the north); it was not ideological or social, not so revolutionary as that of the more industrialized and politically advanced nations who approached China by sea.

At first, contacts between other Europeans and the Chinese were inconsequential. Mindful of the behavior of the Westerners who had plagued her shores in the Age of Exploration, and regarding trade as a privilege to be doled out at her own discretion, Manchu China had imposed stringent restrictions. The foreigners could trade only at Canton and there only with a few so-called Hong merchants, who had a monopoly of foreign trade on the Chinese side. This meant not only that the Europeans were cut off from all other Chinese, but that their bargaining power was undermined, since their choice of action was confined to taking or leaving what the Hong merchants were willing to pay. The foreigners had to reside at the Portuguese leasehold of Macao under Chinese jurisdiction. Only for the duration of the trading season were their commercial agents suffered to move to the trading stations or "factories" at Canton, unarmed and without women or children. In Canton their movements were narrowly circumscribed. They were not permitted to study the Chinese language and were dependent for their needs on the Chinese servants, interpreters, and Hong merchants assigned to them. The system was not without its merits. It gave a certain order to commercial transactions and cushioned the impact of foreign ways. But as traders of the English East India Company replaced the more piratical seamen of the

Age of Exploration, as British commerce increased greatly and the Industrial Revolution multiplied not only the amount of merchandise to be marketed but also the military might of the British Empire, the situation became increasingly unworkable.

The Manchu restrictions were predicated on the inferiority of the long-nosed foreigners. The equality of nations was not a concept readily understandable to the Chinese. For centuries China had been the center of civilization, for centuries China had received tributary missions from other countries. She was willing to permit the continuation of limited trade, but she was not prepared to accept diplomatic relations on an "equal" basis. Sufficient unto herself, she saw no reason to discard or even modify the traditional pattern. But the British, confident in their new prosperity and strength, would no longer be treated as inferior. Furthermore, they wished to be freed from Chinese jurisdiction. Too wide was the gap between Chinese and Western law — not so much in the statutes themselves as in their application. Meanwhile the introduction of opium into the trade with China had poisoned all relations. Not only was the importation of opium a threat to the physical well-being of the Chinese people, but it reversed the balance of trade in favor of the West and, to the dismay of the Chinese officials, caused an outflow of specie from the empire. It was the precipitate destruction of some British opium by a Chinese commissioner that triggered the so-called Opium War in 1839. Nevertheless opium was the major issue from the Chinese point of view only. Equality of treatment, the establishment of diplomatic relations, and the extension of commerce were the issues as far as the British were concerned. The Treaty of Nanking, which the victorious British ultimately imposed on the Manchu government, made no mention of opium.

The thunder of the British cannon ushered in the Age of Imperialism in the Far East. Once victorious, the British did not extend to the Chinese the equality of treatment for which they themselves had fought. The positions were reversed, and the Treaty of Nanking, which ended the war in 1842, was the first of a whole series of "unequal" treaties imposed on China by the Western powers. It compelled China to open five ports to foreign trade, to abolish the Hong merchants' monopoly, and to pay reparations. It provided that official correspondence between the two countries be formulated as between equals, but ceded to Great Britain the island of Hong Kong and provided for the fixing of an import-export tariff rate, which could be modified only by mutual agreement. The full import of this treaty can best be understood if it is kept in mind that Hong Kong is still in British hands (no longer a barren island, but a prosperous citadel of commerce and industry) and that China was prevented from determining her own tariff rate, a major source of governmental income, until as late as 1930.

Having approached China by way of India, where they had lorded over the natives in grand fashion, the British had been particularly incensed by Chinese condescension. The main reason why Britain had spearheaded Western inroads on Chinese sovereignty, however, was that her interests in the China trade were greater than those of anyone else. But the American merchants, whose interest in China antedated the American Revolution, did not wish to be left out.

In 1843, in deference partly to American remonstrance, the British included in a supplementary treaty with China the most-favored-nation clause, which extended to any nation having a most-favored-nation clause in its treaty with China whatever concessions China might make to any other power. At first glance this clause may have appeared eminently fair. It was actually welcomed by China, which, if open it must, preferred to open equally to all in the hope of applying the time-tested Chinese stratagem of playing barbarians against barbarians. But in time the most-favored-nation clause evolved into the most devilish device of imperialism, extorting concessions from China without granting anything in return and pitting China against the whole imperialist world.

The first American treaty with China was signed in 1844 at Wanghia. It included a most-favored-nation clause and clearly stated the principle of extraterritoriality, by which Americans (and other foreigners whose treaties so provided) remained immune from Chinese jurisdiction in China. However desirable this provision may have been at the time, in view of the gulf between Chinese and Western legal concepts, it constituted another infringement on Chinese sovereignty. Like the tariff restrictions, it lasted well into the modern era — indeed until 1943. Thus the humiliations of the Age of Imperialism, reaching back even to the first treaties of Great Britain and the United States with China, are fresh in Chinese minds today. They have become the springboard of twentieth-century nationalism, an indelible mark on the psyche of China's modern leaders, a key to understanding Chinese disdain for Western legal and moral protestations.

The American treaty provided for possible revision in twelve years. When at the end of that term the Manchu officials refused to enter upon discussions, the British, to whom the provisions had been extended by virtue of the most-favored-nation clause, resorted to force again. A pretext was found in the boarding by Manchu officials of a Chinese vessel, registered in Hong Kong and flying the British flag, and the removal of Chinese crew members. Though the British had insisted on their own right to do the same to American vessels even after the War of 1812, they professed to be outraged by the Manchu action. They were joined by the French, a missionary of whom had been executed by a Chinese magistrate for penetrating into the interior of the country, and the combined Anglo-French forces attacked the Chinese by sea. Blasting their way up to Tientsin, they obtained new concessions from the Chinese. The Americans and the Russians refrained from use of force, but their negotiators followed close on the heels of the English and French, chugging along on a steamer flying the American and Russian flags, ready to sign agreements embodying the concessions extorted by English and French guns. It was this sort of American policy in the Far East, together with the Open Door doctrine, to be discussed later, that has been aptly labeled a "me-too policy" or, better still, "hitchhiking imperialism." It was

this American approach that prompted a Chinese observer to re-
mark, "Better enemies like the British, than friends like the
Americans."

The treaties of Tientsin, concluded in 1858, legalized the
importation of opium, sanctioned the residence of Western diplomats in the capital of Peking, and stipulated the toleration
of Christian missionaries and converts. It was not the Church's
fault that it had gained entry in such fashion. Yet this was to be
its Achilles' heel. In the public mind of China the missionary
movement and Western imperialism were fatally linked.

China had resisted relations with the West. Forced to sign
treaties, she hindered the implementing of them by non-coop-
eration, sabotage, and violence. Chinese resentment was aggravated by the sanctimonious arrogance of some of the foreigners;
it was fanned by superstition and fantastic rumors, often spread
by designing officials. The foreigners proved handy political
whipping boys, on whom the failures of the Chinese government could be blamed. The infamous Tientsin Massacre of 1870,
in which a Catholic orphanage was destroyed and many Christians were murdered by a lynch mob, was all too typical an
example of how then (as now) a few half-truths sufficed to transform the mistrust of an uneducated public into violent antifor-
eign action. Bent on saving souls, the Catholics paid Chinese
parents to bring their critically ill children to the orphanage, so
that they could be properly prepared for death and the after-
life. All that the general public knew, however, was that an
unusually high percentage of children sent to the orphanage died.
When the inmates of the orphanage were further decimated by
an epidemic, rumors spread that the nuns were murdering the
Chinese children, and the mob went into action while the officials looked the other way.

The repeated humiliation of the Manchu government at the
hands of the Western powers did much to undermine its prestige in China. But its weakness was to a large extent internal.
The Manchu dynasty had ruled already for two centuries, nearly
the average life span of a dynasty in China. With time, the ability and vigor of its emperors had declined, undermined by the

distractions of a luxurious court and the hereditary principle of succession. The organization and experience of its military forces had been eroded by generations of peace, and Chinese scholars, in spite of Manchu tenure of key positions, had gained control of most of the administration. The Manchus themselves had become completely Sinicized. Although military conquerors, they came to terms with the essentially antimilitary Confucianism. Highly conscious of being foreigners, they sought acceptance by being more strict and inflexible in adhering to Chinese ways than the Chinese themselves; and the latter, since their liberation from the Mongol tyranny, had become almost slavishly addicted to the past. All this is basic to understanding China's failure in the nineteenth century to rise to the challenge of the West.

Moral superiority and aesthetic finesse were useless weapons in the Age of Imperialism. No Mahatma Gandhi could have stemmed the Western tide in the nineteenth century. Military might was the source of respect if not the criterion of civilization. Certainly it was the only means of defense. And military might, by this time, meant more than sheer manpower; it meant a navy and an army equipped with new weapons, a military machine built on the foundations of an industrial society. But the Chinese bureaucrats, who had spent many years in arduous study of the Chinese classics, had no admiration for the death-dealing instruments of the West. Even had they appreciated the full lethal significance of industrialized militarism, they could not have been expected to commit professional suicide by casting aside their laboriously acquired Confucian learning, the basis of their official position. On the other hand, China lacked the elements for private industrialization. Land and usury absorbed most investments; there was no surplus from foreign trade, such as Great Britain had acquired; and, in general, commercial success was sought not by improving a product but by obtaining a government monopoly thereof. Confucianism offered every precedent for government initiative and participation in national economic development, but the government was not yet sufficiently alert to the needs of a new age.

Over the centuries China had been held together by adherence to a common culture, but there was no nationalism in the modern sense. Confucianism was at once universal and particular. It was universal in that it dealt with human values, with human relations, applicable to all ages and societies. It was particular in that it emphasized filial piety, family obligations, and loyalty to one's master, not to the nation. The Western powers did not really war with China as an entity. They fought now against one locality, now against another, while maintaining relatively peaceful relations elsewhere.

In the middle of the nineteenth century the disunity of China and the bankruptcy of Manchu rule were accentuated by the outbreak of the T'ai P'ing Rebellion, the greatest civil war of all times. For over fourteen years, from 1850 to 1864, China was torn by strife. Some twenty million people perished and many of the most prosperous regions were laid waste. The end of the Manchu dynasty seemed in sight.

Like many earlier uprisings, the T'ai P'ing Rebellion, in addition to its economic and social causes, had a religious tinge. This time, however, the tinge was not Taoist or Buddhist, but Christian. Hung Hsiu-ch'üan, the leader of the T'ai P'ing, was a despondent would-be scholar-official, who, unsuccessful in his examinations, appears to have suffered a nervous breakdown, during which he had a vision. Interpreting it upon his recovery in the light of some Christian tracts which he had acquired from a missionary, he launched a crusade against the worship of the devil. When the government sought to interfere with his destruction of temples, he turned against the Manchu dynasty, assumed the title of Heavenly King, and proclaimed the imminence of the reign of Great Peace (T'ai P'ing).

Hung's study of Christian doctrine and the far-reaching reform program of his rebellion at first appealed to the Westerners, who themselves were at war with the Manchus in 1858-60. The T'ai P'ing inveighed against foot binding, slavery, arranged marriage, concubinage, and the use of opium; they advocated redistribution of land, equality of men and women, and equal educational opportunities for all. But they failed to attract the Chinese intellectuals, and lacked competent and united leadership. Furthermore, the Christian elements were too tenuous to give direction to the movement: the veneer of Christian borrowing was thin and was decidedly unorthodox, since Hung regarded himself as the younger brother of Jesus Christ. When the T'ai P'ing, in spite of early overtures to the West, became as arrogant as the Manchus and more reckless and dangerous to foreign interests, the Westerners rallied to the Manchu side. While themselves still fighting the Manchus, they helped to defeat the T'ai P'ing with the "Ever Victorious Army," recruited from among Western adventurers.

The T'ai P'ing Rebellion did incalculable damage to an already weak economy and shaky government. The aid of the Westerners in defeating the T'ai P'ing prolonged Manchu rule on "borrowed time." It postponed the inevitable collapse of the dynasty to a period when, as fate would have it, the usual pains of dynastic change-over and the weak, inexperienced attempts at republican government were compounded by the infusion of yet another Western heresy — Communism. The Communists, incidentally, view the T'ai P'ing Rebellion as the beginning of the Chinese Revolution and point to Western support of the Manchus as proof of historical Western opposition to the democratic aspirations of the Chinese people.

The ruler with whom the Westerners had to deal primarily in the years following the T'ai P'ing Rebellion was Tz'u Hsi, the Empress Dowager, popularly known as the "Old Buddha." The widow of Emperor Hsien Feng, she guided China from 1861 until 1908, indirectly as regent through a succession of imperial puppets, or directly if the occasion demanded. She was a remarkable woman, energetic, ambitious, and skillful in court politics, but she was also grossly superstitious, given to indecision, and unable to understand the scope and significance of the foreign threat.

In 1894–95 the Manchu empire received its severest jolt since the T'ai P'ing Rebellion. In a revival of the age-old dispute with Japan over control of Korea, the Manchu forces were decisively beaten, and China was compelled to make humiliating concessions, including the cession of Formosa (Taiwan) and the

Pescadores islands and the payment of a large indemnity. The makings of the Sino-Japanese War will be related in the section on Japan; it is enough to mention here that Japanese ambitions were abetted needlessly by Manchu reluctance to act with determination, and in time, to assert China's rights and live up to China's responsibilities in Korea and other outlying regions during the 1870's and 1880's. What concerns us at this point is the impact of the defeat on China itself and on the general course of Far Eastern international relations.

In China, the victory of Japan showed the effective use to which Western arms could be put by a non-Western nation. It gave an important stimulus, at least in some quarters, to follow in Japanese footsteps and adopt Western technology. Abroad, the defeat of the Chinese colossus by tiny Japan reversed the whole power picture; Japan now took the place of China as a possible ally in Far Eastern schemes. Heretofore Far Eastern international relations had been steered almost exclusively by the policies of the colonial powers and the reaction of the Oriental governments thereto; now Far Eastern international relations became part of world politics, with an Asian nation, Japan, setting the course for some of the major developments. Most important of all, China, which so far had found at least some protection in its apparently great potential power, now was laid bare to the fangs of territorial demands.

The Treaty of Shimonoseki, which ended the Sino-Japanese War in 1895, recognized Korean independence, and in addition granted to Japan not only the above-mentioned islands (Formosa and the Pescadores) but also the South Manchurian Liaotung peninsula, including Port Arthur. This foothold on the Asian mainland, however, the Western powers would not tolerate. Russia (which had begun construction of a railroad across the continent to the Pacific), together with Germany and France, intervened with the categoric demand that Japan accept a higher financial indemnity instead. Japan backed down, but the seeds of an armed clash between Russia and Japan had been sown, the more so as Russia, having already obtained valuable territorial concessions in the north in 1858 and 1860, annexed in

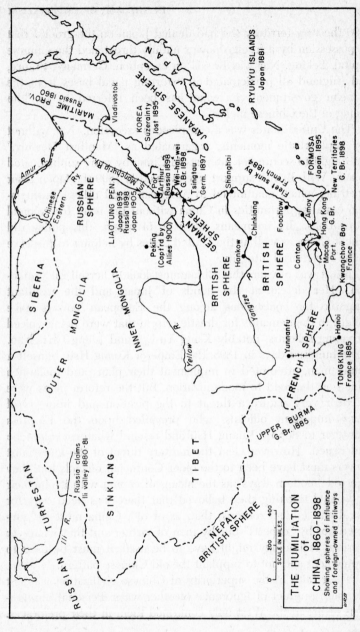

From Alfred Crofts and Percy Buchanan, *A History of the Far East*; copyright, 1958, Longmans, Green & Co., Inc.

THE HUMILIATION of CHINA 1860-1898
Showing spheres of influence and foreign-owned railways

SCALE IN MILES
0   200   400

SIBERIA

TURKESTAN

RUSSIAN Ili R.

Russia claims Ili valley 1880-81

SINKIANG

TIBET

NEPAL BRITISH SPHERE

OUTER MONGOLIA

INNER MONGOLIA

Yellow R.

UPPER BURMA G. Br. 1885

FRENCH SPHERE

Yunnanfu

Hanoi

TONGKING France 1885

BRITISH SPHERE

Yangtze R.

Hankow

Chinkiang

Foochow

Canton

Macao Port.

Hong Kong G. Br.

Kwangchow Bay France

Amoy

New Territories G. Br. 1898

FORMOSA Japan 1895

Fleet sunk by French 1884

Shanghai

BRITISH SPHERE

GERMAN SPHERE

Tsingtau Germ. 1897

Peking (Capt'd by Allies 1900)

Wei-hai-wei G.Br. 1898

Port Arthur Russia 1898

LIAOTUNG PEN. Japan 1895 Russia 1898 Japan 1905

Manchurian Ry.

RUSSIAN SPHERE

Chinese Eastern Ry.

Amur R.

MARITIME PROV. Russia 1860

Vladivostok

KOREA Suzerainty lost 1895

JAPANESE SPHERE

JAPAN

RYUKYU ISLANDS Japan 1881

1898 the very territory she had denied Japan on the ground that its possession by a foreign power unduly threatened the Chinese capital, Peking. Nor was Russia an exception. Germany, France, and England all participated in extorting naval bases from the Manchu government, in what has been referred to as "the slicing of the Chinese melon."

The United States was a conspicuous exception. Not without her imperialistic moments, sugarcoated as "Manifest Destiny," she sought to secure her interests in China by more sophisticated means. With British support, she evolved in 1899 the Open Door Doctrine, which guaranteed to American (and other) businessmen equal opportunities in China without the need for colonial acquisitions. By no means altruistic in origin, this policy did benefit China as well as the United States by helping to preserve China's territorial integrity.

But it was obvious that China must look to herself for protection. Her defeat at the hands of Japan and the resultant scramble for concessions among the European powers gave weight to the demands for drastic reform that were being voiced by young scholars, notably K'ang Yu-wei and Liang Ch'i-ch'ao. For a hundred days in 1898, the Emperor Kuang Hsü, himself a young man, attempted to implement their plans and to launch China on the road to modernization. But the reform plans were by their very nature a threat to the position and interests of many important officials, who prevailed upon the Empress Dowager to depose Kuang Hsü and rescind whatever edicts he had issued. However clear the military threat of the imperialist powers must have been to the older Confucian officials too, they rejected "modern ways" as the means of coping with it. In their traditional thinking they believed that there was need only for moral and ethical reforms; that, as of old, China must be governed not by "experts" but by men of virtue; and that whatever Western technology might have to be used, it must be used to supplement and not to supplant the old Chinese pattern.

Their faith in the superiority of Chinese civilization was not the mere product of ignorance of other ways. Personal observations of life in the West only confirmed them in their prejudices.

The following entries from the diary of a Chinese traveler were characteristic of the Confucian cast of mind:

China has all four seasons and the climate is proportionally distributed. In parts of the West the heat and cold are unseasonable, the winter and summer change their normal order, and there are spots that from ancient down to modern times have never had frost or snow. . . .

As to human affairs, China emphasizes human relationships and honors benevolence and righteousness. In the West, on the contrary, a son does not take care of his father, a minister cheats his emperor, a wife is more honored than a husband; thus the bond of the three relationships is broken. Because the proper relationship between husband and wife is not cultivated, the marriage ceremony is neglected. As soon as a girl is twenty-one years old she is permitted to find a husband whom she likes, and there are those who make many selections or trials before they make a match. They do not consider sexual relations preceding marriage a shame. Beautiful young girls are seeking for males everywhere; the hoary-headed and the widows can invite male companions as they like. The customs are bad to such a degree! . . .

As to other customs, the residence of the emperor is the same as that of the ordinary people except that it is a little larger, and it lacks an awe-inspiring appearance and dignity. The pictures of the emperor and the empress are hung up at random in the markets for sale and people can purchase them as toys. Thus there is no distinction between the noble and the mean. . . .

Speaking about official costumes, except in one country, Turkey, where the costume is strange, all other nations are the same. The noble and the mean use the same style, which makes it difficult to tell who is honorable and who is lowly. In the summertime there is no linen or silk to make their bodies comfortable, and in winter there are rarely furs or padded coats to dress their bodies. They have to go to the trouble of taking a carriage or a horse, but do not have the comfort of sedan chairs. The skirts of their women are seven feet long, only good for sweeping dust. The bed curtain is hung ten feet high but it is hard to keep mosquitoes away.

As for food, there is no difference between winter and summer; they always sip cold water and juice. They cannot appreciate the culinary art, but like butter and mutton ribs. The amount of food served at meals is small, and they use many different kinds of utensils to cause servants a good deal of work. The kinds of soap are very limited. Delicious things are completely lacking.

In government, their taxes since antiquity have been unprecedentedly heavy and numerous. There is actually a levy of taxes of certain amounts according to the value of commodities. If smuggling is detected, the tax on the smuggled article is increased ten or a hundred times as a fine. In some places there is a land tax. Some have a poll tax, or property tax, or tax on trademarks. The government takes money from people insatiably. How can the people bear it? Moreover, they worship their unorthodox religion and allow the Christian clergy to overrun the country, exhausting all the people's money in building churches, thus spending useful funds for a useless purpose.

As for the law, it has no articles for punishing adultery; a wife can have a concubine [i.e., a lover] and can accuse her husband. This is even more ridiculous. Apart from these there are other things which they improperly turn upside down. Their prisons, for example, are as comfortable as the Kingdom of Heaven. It is not very easy for people to maintain their living, because the cost of food and utensils is as high as that of precious jewels. The five relationships are not cultivated, the five kinds of grains are incomplete, hundreds of herbs are unknown to them and hundreds of grasses or flowers are not fragrant. . . .[1]

In 1898 China was not yet ready for reform. K'ang Yu-wei and Liang Ch'i-ch'ao had to flee for their lives and lay the foundations of a more liberal modern Chinese tradition through their writing in Japan.

Meanwhile the conduct of the Western powers in China, the activities of the missionaries and of their converts, and especially the attitude of the Christian converts toward their fellow countrymen, not only in terms of haughtiness but of separation from the community and reliance on Western protection, steadily increased popular antagonism towards Christianity and the West until at the turn of the century it exploded in the Boxer Rebellion (1899–

[1] Ssu-yu Teng, John K. Fairbank, and others, *China's Response to the West. A Documentary Survey 1839–1923* (Cambridge: Harvard University Press, 1954), pp. 184–185.

1900). Not initiated by the Manchu court, in fact at first hostile to it, the Boxer movement was soon exploited and used by the court, the conservatives wishing to restore China's safety through isolation. "Get rid of the foreigners and all the difficulties will have been overcome," became the slogan. No doubt the foreigners had but themselves to blame for the eruption of Chinese hostility. At the same time, the deftness of the government in exploiting antiforeignism in its own interest was but a portent of the gigantic hate campaigns of our own day.

The Boxer movement was widespread, reaching its greatest extent in Shantung province. It was not exclusively Boxer in inception. The Society of Harmonious Fists, as the Boxers were properly called, was merely the most important of a number of revolutionary groups. They murdered many Christians and besieged the foreign embassies, to whose rescue an international expeditionary force had to be dispatched. The foreign troops proceeded on Peking with much wanton destruction; the Japanese, in this their first exposure of their armies to the Western eye, conducted themselves with perhaps the greatest restraint. But though the Boxer uprising was widespread, it was not a national uprising. Many of the officials refused to carry out the orders to drive or try to drive the foreigners into the sea. As the foreign expedition approached, the Empress Dowager and the court fled the capital, to return later in great humiliation.

Among the various terms that the Chinese and Manchus had to accept, in consequence of the rebellion, were the establishment of a regular Foreign Office, the modification of the ceremonial used in the reception at court of foreign envoys, and the payment of a sizable financial indemnity. (The United States later remitted part of its share as support for the modern education of Chinese students.) But more important than these and other formal concessions was the obvious failure of the reactionary policy of the Empress Dowager, and the resulting introduction of an era of conservative reform. This program of reform was given added stimulus by Japan's defeat of Russia, and will be discussed in Part Three.

JAPAN

The Age of Imperialism left a very different mark on Japan than on the rest of Asia. In part this may have been due to British preoccupation with India and China, but principally it was due to conditions within Japan. Unlike Manchu China, Japan had a native government. Virtually the entire ruling class, moreover, was military, owing its position not to learning but to birth. Compared with China's Confucian ruling class, it was better prepared intellectually and less hampered by considerations of personal success to appreciate the nature of the Western threat and to cope with it accordingly. Furthermore, Japan was not so self-sufficient as China. Not only did she have more of a tradition and craving for foreign products and ideas, but the needs of her large capital city of Edo (Tokyo), of her rapidly expanding internal trade and money economy, and of her growing merchant class were hampered by the policy of seclusion. As we have seen, Japan's self-imposed isolation from the Western world had not been absolute. Through the "window on the West" at Deshima, where the Dutch were suffered to maintain a

trading post, the Japanese had kept an eye on the progress of
world events; and after the ban on Western books was relaxed,
a trickle of European learning, particularly in the sciences, filtered into the country through students of the Dutch language.

Pressure gradually mounted within, as well as without, for the
reopening of Japan. If the shogunate tried as stubbornly as the
Manchu government to delay the conclusion of treaties with the
West, it was moved almost as much by fear of showing weakness
at home as by fear of showing weakness abroad. The big difference was that the Japanese, familiar with developments on
the continent, yielded to the inevitable with the determination
to make the best of a bad situation, adopt the superior military
ways of the West, and recoup their position at a more favorable
time.

Western attempts to reopen Japan go back to the end of the
seventeenth century, when the discovery of a Japanese castaway
by a Russian explorer stirred Peter the Great's interest and
sparked a whole series of Russian efforts to establish relations
with the Japanese empire. In 1739 the Russians first reached
Japan. In 1792 and in 1804 they entered into protracted negotiations in Japan. But the Japanese government, after considerable
deliberation, reaffirmed its determination to remain isolated.
Several incidents followed, some violent, but Russo-Japanese relations remained confined essentially to illicit trade on the Kuril
islands, mostly through Ainu middlemen.

Russian interest in Japan is not surprising. Russia was Japan's
nearest Western neighbor. At the same time, Japan was nearer
to the eastern extremities of the Russian empire than were
Russia's own European centers of production, and, owing to her
economic advancement, held out hope of becoming a natural
source of supplies for eastern Siberia. With the pressure of
rival powers on the tottering Manchu empire in the Age of
Imperialism, Russian interest in Japan became more strategic:
Japan was important to Russia as a potential source of supplies,
as an ice-free naval base for operations against China and for
patrolling the Russian shores, and as a coaling station on the way
to Alaska.

Japan's location between the Asian mainland and the North American continent attracted also the interest of the United States, whose push toward and across the Pacific Ocean from the opposite direction resembled that of Russia in many respects. American interest in Japan dated back to the extension of the Pacific Northwest fur trade and had accelerated concurrently with progress in whale fishing, commerce with China, and steam navigation. It had been intensified by Japanese imprisonment of shipwrecked Americans and by apprehension lest Russia establish herself in Japan and gain control of the commerce of the Pacific.

Like the Russians, the Americans made several fruitless attempts to open Japan; but at last, in 1854, while the Russians negotiated in another part of Japan, the American efforts were crowned with success. Commodore Matthew Calbraith Perry signed the first Western treaty with Japan.

The nature of the opening of Japan is important. There had been no fighting; Japanese and Westerners alike had conducted themselves with restraint. But Perry had not been received with open arms; his words and the very presence in Edo Bay of his mighty fleet (ultimately nine men-of-war, manned by almost one quarter of the U.S. Navy) had been a very definite threat of force. As the Japanese yielded, they did so with significant mental reservations, agreeing generally with the line of thought of Abe Masahiro, President of the Cabinet:

> As we are not the equals of foreigners in the mechanical arts, let us have intercourse with foreign countries, learn their drill and tactics, and when we have made the nation as united as one family, we shall be able to go abroad and give lands in foreign countries to those who have distinguished themselves in battle; the soldiers will vie with one another in displaying their intrepidity, and it will not be too late to declare war. Now we shall have to defend ourselves against these foreign enemies skilled in the use of mechanical appliances, with our soldiers whose military skill has considerably diminished during a long peace of three hundred years, and we certainly could not feel sure of victory, especially in a naval war.[1]

[1] Ernest Satow, *Japan 1853–1864 (Genji yume monogatari)* (Tokyo, 1905), pp. 5–8.

Commodore Perry's treaty and the treaties concluded shortly by the other Western powers were not much more than shipwreck conventions. It remained for another American, Townsend Harris, without visible means of military support, to open Japan to Western commerce (1858). It was a great victory for the whole West, but again the attitude of the Japanese must not be overlooked. In his attempt to gain imperial approval of the treaties of 1858, Lord Hotta Masayoshi, Prime Minister and later Foreign Minister of the shogunate, argued that "in establishing relations with foreign countries, the object should always be kept in view of laying a foundation for securing the hegemony over all nations"; that, having developed her resources and military strength, Japan, in execution of the power and authority deputed to her by the Spirit of Heaven, should become the champion of international interests, so that "the nations of the world will come to look up to our Emperor as the Great Ruler of all the nations, and they will come to follow our policy and submit themselves to our judgment."

The apprehensiveness of the shogunate in opening Japan had been justified. Foreign trade, in its early stages, did more harm than good; the conduct of many Western merchants and seamen was deplorable; and the ill effects of this intercourse, notably the rise in the cost of living, aroused public resentment against both the foreigners and the government. The treaties themselves became a political club, wielded with effect by the imperial opponents of the shogunate. The murder in 1859 of two Russian mariners and the following year of Lord Ii Naosuke, leading official of the shogunate, marked the beginning of a period of assassinations which, in 1868, culminated in the overthrow of the shogunate.

The transition was facilitated by the common realization that Japan must stand united under one government in the face of the Western threat — twice in 1863 Western gunboats had avenged anti-European acts — and by the deaths of the two major rivals, Shogun Tokugawa Iemochi and Emperor Komei, in the same year (1867). Called upon by the spokesman of the imperial forces (primarily the feudal clans of western Japan) to return the reins of government to the emperor "voluntarily,"

lest a civil war leave Japan open to foreign inroads, the new
shogun complied. Fighting did break out subsequently, when
the Tokugawa realized that they were to be shorn not only of
their authority but also of their lands and influence. Their opposition was short-lived, however, and on January 3, 1868, the young
Emperor Meiji proclaimed the restoration of imperial rule.

"Meiji" was the emperor's reign name. It meant "enlightened rule." Uninhibited by the antiforeignism of his late
father, the fifteen-year-old monarch proceeded to set down in
the famous Charter Oath of Five Articles the principles of his
"enlightened rule" and the direction which modern Japan was to
take during his long reign (1868–1912):

1. An assembly widely convoked shall be established, and thus
   great stress shall be laid upon public discussion.
2. The welfare of the whole nation shall be promoted by the
   everlasting efforts of both the governing and the governed
   classes.
3. All subjects, civil and military officers, as well as other people,
   shall do their best and never grow weary in accomplishing their
   legitimate purposes.
4. All absurd usages shall be abandoned; justice and righteousness
   shall regulate all actions.
5. Knowledge shall be sought for all over the world and thus shall
   be strengthened the foundation of the Imperial polity.[2]

The aspirations of these articles have not lost their appeal with
time. It was to the Charter Oath that Emperor Showa (Hirohito) turned in his New Year's Day Rescript of 1946 as the basis
for a new and peaceful Japan.

In line with his determination to modernize Japan, Emperor
Meiji moved from the ancient imperial city of Kyoto to Edo,
renaming it Tokyo, the "Eastern Capital."

The Restoration was not the work of one man. It was not
radical; not the product of popular upheaval. The restoration of
imperial rule did not actually mean the passing of absolute

2 W. W. McLaren, "Japanese Government Documents," *Transactions of
the Asiatic Society of Japan*, vol. 42 (Tokyo, 1914), p. 8.

personal power and initiative into the hands of Emperor Meiji. By and large he acted on the advice of his ministers and counsellors. The government, as in the past, was in the hands of men from the leading clans, in this case primarily Satsuma and Choshu. The samurai, who had effected the Restoration, continued to mastermind the course of Japanese history for the rest of their lives. Nor was the Restoration accomplished overnight. It extended over a period of about twenty years, culminating in the Constitution of 1889.

The necessity of strengthening the country without delay, in order to avoid the consequences of weakness, so tragically evident at the time in China, forced the Japanese to give full priority to economic reforms. They modernized with startling speed. Many factors were in their favor. Their country was small; it had a rich tradition of borrowing; it had a public relatively disciplined to following the dictates of its leaders. But the very speed of the modernization, however admirable, dictated the character of Japan's industrialization, which in turn gave birth to many of Japan's future problems.

Japan did not have a surplus of capital in private hands. As in China, land, with its high rental income, was the most attractive investment. This was the more so because private industry could not profitably compete with the products of foreign countries, in view of Japan's limited technical experience and the tariff restrictions imposed by the Western powers (similar to those imposed on China). Thus the government had to step in, and government leadership and participation in industry became the foremost characteristic of Japanese industrialization. The commercial families who had helped to finance the Restoration were drawn into cooperative ventures with the government; once an industry had been firmly established, they often received it at a fraction of its value.

In 1870 most feudal lords, conscious that it was imperative for Japan to have a strong sovereign and assured of financial support by the government, voluntarily transferred their fiefs to the emperor. In 1871 feudalism was officially abolished, the various clans being converted into prefectures. In return for the surrender of their fiefs the lords received a pension. When several years later the government made a lump sum settlement, commuting the pensions into government bonds and cash, the landed aristocrats were suddenly transformed into capitalists. As the former lords became big businessmen and the lower samurai continued in their employ or in the employ of government-sponsored projects, they injected into the Japanese business world an ultra-conservative strain, which inhibited opposition to militarism and government autocracy. Old feudal values and social standards persisted in civilian garb, with the sword-wielding police force, the refuge of many ex-samurai, in a position of undue popular respect. The close tie between the government and the landed, financial, and military interests was the second major characteristic of Japanese industrialism.

The development of Japanese industry was not "natural," in response to the demands of the economy. It was a forced development to meet a military need, and the government, with this in mind, emphasized heavy and strategic industries. But the agriculture and the household industries of Japan constituted an inadequate foundation for the grandiose economic structure erected by the government. The unsound development of the economy was the third characteristic of Japanese industrialization.

Related to this was another factor of great consequence. Desperately short of capital, and willing to make but the most sparing use of foreign aid lest outside interference be invited, Japan could pay only the lowest wages to her workers. This low wage-scale (plus high rent and land taxes) deprived Japan, as her industries developed further, of a market for her own goods at home. Thus the fourth characteristic of Japan's industrialization was her dependence on foreign markets, a dependence which made her unduly vulnerable to foreign tariff policies and misled her ultimately to attempt to secure markets by conquest. Japan's experience casts a disturbing light on the frantic industrialization of technologically backward countries in our own day.

Because political reforms were left until after the economic reforms had become well established, economic measures could be carried out with little political opposition. At the same time this gave the ruling oligarchy the opportunity to consolidate its position, and when political reforms were finally made they were less modern in fact than in appearance. Like China, Japan was saddled with "unequal" treaties that infringed on her tariff and judicial powers. To rid herself of the restrictions of extra-territoriality, Japan had to prove her "enlightenment" to Western satisfaction by the emulation of Western ways. Japanese efforts were intensified by the fact that the Japanese, less selfsure than the Chinese, had a dread of being ridiculed. Without losing respect for the intrinsic values of their own culture they accepted Western customs and institutions, if not as a necessary evil, at least without inner conviction and more in letter than in spirit. As a result, in many respects Japan became more modern in appearance than in character. For example, the educational system was remodeled after Western fashion in organization and teaching methods, but remained thoroughly Japanese in basic policy and purpose, training for the needs of the state, and stressing loyalty to the state and to the ancient values of Japan.

The structure of the Japanese government as it was developed in the late 1870's and 1880's, and formulated in the Constitution of 1889, was deceptively Western in form and terminology, but Japanese in actual operation. Not theories or institutions but classes of people — aristocrats, bureaucrats, militarists, and politicians — dominated the scene. Thus the course of government was shaped to a large extent by extra-constitutional factors. For example, no mention was made in the Constitution of 1889 of the *genro* or elder statesmen. These were the men (all of them, with one exception, from the powerful former fiefs of Satsuma and Choshu) who had carried through the Restoration, and they retained until their death the real power of government. To give another example, in accordance with a pre-constitutional decree which was not superseded by the constitution, the important cabinet positions of Minister of War and Minister of the Navy had to be filled by, respectively, generals and admirals on active duty. This meant that every cabinet was dependent on the support of the army and the navy; that, being able to precipitate the fall of any government by recalling these ministers to active duty, the army and the navy were in an unusual position to influence the government. Within the constitution itself there were provisions which prolonged the dominance of the clan statesmen and hamstrung the development of party government. But the clan statesmen proved unable to keep the military in check, and the latter repeatedly embarked on imperialistic ventures, dragging along an often unwilling but impotent government.

When the Western powers opened Japan in the 1850's, they uncorked the jinni of expansion which the Tokugawa shogunate had bottled up for over two centuries. Age-old interests and ambitions revived, as the descendants of those who had withstood Mongol invasions, raided the coasts of China, overrun Korea, and carried their reputation as valiant and ferocious fighting men to the shores of Southeast Asia, girded their strength for national survival. In foreign policy, as in the modernization of their country, the Japanese had no definite plan. They had the courage to experiment, and felt their way by a policy of trial and error. In foreign policy, as in every other area, the Japanese resorted to Western methods, not only to combat the West with its own weapons, but to shroud their own ancient ambitions in a cloak of modernity.

In 1870, only twelve years after they themselves had bowed reluctantly to Western demands of trade, the Japanese called on China to establish commercial relations with them, insisting that in the modern world there was no longer "near nor far." The treaty which was finally concluded in 1871 contained reciprocal rights; from the standpoint of Sino-Japanese relations, it was a treaty of perfect equality. Yet the Japanese attitude during the negotiations and the public reaction in Japan to the final treaty made it clear that Japan aspired to more than equality with China. She wanted to be on an equal footing with the Western powers in China. Equality with the West became Japan's primary objective, indeed her obsession, and to attain it she chose to follow in the footsteps of Western imperialism. In 1874 the Japanese sent an expeditionary force to Formosa, as much to give the restless military something to do and get them out of the country as to punish the natives for the mistreatment of shipwrecked Liu Ch'iu and Japanese sailors, when the Manchus, to whom the island belonged, failed to take prompt action. But the ambitions of the military were not allayed. For two more decades the government struggled to restrain them, lest the economic development of Japan be sidetracked, but by 1894 it loosened the reins and Japan clashed head-on with China.

The Sino-Japanese War of 1894–95 was ignited over Korea. Many a time the ancient kingdom of Korea had survived foreign invasion and recovered with renewed vigor, but not after the devastating campaigns of the Japanese in the late sixteenth century and the Manchu conquest in the early seventeenth century. Isolated by the Manchus from the rest of the world, Korea lived in a state of suspended development, failing to keep up with the march of time. By the late nineteenth century the country was backward, weak, and ill-governed — a natural object of imperialistic contention.

The importance of Korea lay in her geographical position. She was a bridge between the Asian continent and Japan, a two-way street affording passage for invasion armies in either direction. At the same time, her ice-free harbors could be used the year round and afforded better protection than the harbors of Russia to the north. In the hands of Japan, Korea formed the closing link in a chain that could block a Russian outlet to the Pacific. It was therefore in the interest of each of the three East Asian powers, China, Japan, and Russia, that neither of the other two control Korea. A strong and independent Korea might have served as a stabilizing factor in this three-cornered rivalry, but Chinese, Japanese, and Russian efforts to pressure a weak and reluctant Korea into reforms necessary even for her own strength and independence created more problems than they solved.

Throughout, Japan held the initiative. In 1876 a Japanese

squadron opened Korea in Perry-like fashion. In 1881 Japan obtained further trade concessions through military pressure following an attack by a Korean mob on the Japanese legation. In 1884 the Japanese were implicated in the assassination of Korean ministers who opposed Japanese-style reforms; attained temporary control over the king; and after a clash with Chinese troops, gained further concessions in Korea. But neither Japan nor China was ready for a showdown. To protect the peninsula from each other, they provided for the build-up of a Korean army by a third power, thereby practically inviting the spread of Russian influence. By 1894, however, Japan and China were ready for a test of strength. On the outbreak of a rebellion in Korea and a call for help to China by the Korean king, both sent troops to Korea and locked in war. The position of China was not without fault (for example, she had failed to notify Japan of the troop dispatch, as agreed previously), but Japan was bent on war. The bellicosity of the Japanese military was joined by the desire of the civilian bureaucracy to frustrate the opposition of the rising political parties by uniting the country in a common cause, and was further bolstered by Japan's acceptance of the European theorem that security of economic interests in a region presupposed political entrenchment.

The war was as brief as it was decisive. The Japanese destroyed the Chinese fleet, overran Korea, Manchuria, and Formosa, and were about to push into China proper when the Manchus sued for peace. As already mentioned, the treaty of Shimonoseki, which ended the war, provided for the full independence of Korea, the cession of Formosa and the Pescadores islands to Japan, the opening of additional Chinese ports to commerce, and the payment of an indemnity. The treaty provided also for the cession of the Liaotung peninsula, but, as we have seen, this was blocked by Russia, Germany, and France, and Japan had to accept instead an increased indemnity.

The effects of Japan's victory were far-reaching. On the international level, she replaced China as the leading nation of the Far East. On the national level, the military had been proved right. As a result of the large indemnity, the war had literally "paid," and the armed forces had new funds for increased expansion. The effects of the three-power intervention also were grave. Japan learned that in the West, in the Age of Imperialism at least, might was right, and that Russia stood yet in the path of her continental aspirations.

The sequence of events from the three-power intervention to the outbreak of the Russo-Japanese War was not inevitable, however. Both in Japan and in Russia there were statesmen of note who argued that the two powers had more to gain by making common cause than by opposing each other. As late as 1901 such a Russo-Japanese agreement was a possibility. But the Russian Far Eastern policy degenerated with the rise to influence of reckless militarists who had nothing but contempt for the "yellow macacos" and cold-shouldered a Japanese proposal to delineate spheres of influence, with Manchuria under Russian ascendancy and Korea under Japanese. Japan decided, therefore, to strike before the completion of the railroad across Manchuria should allow Russia to consolidate her position in the Far East.

In the three-power intervention of 1895 Germany had played more than a secondary role. The German government had encouraged Russian entanglement in the Far East in order to limit Russian capabilities in Europe. But Russian expansion and discrimination against Western business in Manchuria endangered the interests of Great Britain, Russia's major European rival in Asia, and in 1902 Great Britain concluded with Japan an alliance which in effect islolated Russia from the military support of a third power in her struggle with Japan.

In a spectacular series of victories in 1904–05 (similar to the early Japanese successes in World War II) Japan defeated what until then had been regarded as the major land power of the West. Abetted though her victory had been by revolution in Russia and by American mediation leading to a peace treaty before Japan had exhausted her straining resources, it was nonetheless victory, decisive and world-shaking. The provisions of the Treaty of Portsmouth, which terminated the war in 1905, were of regional significance. Japan's paramount interests in

Korea were recognized; Russian rights in the Liaotung peninsula and in the southern half of Sakhalin were ceded to Japan;
and Russian influence in Manchuria was curbed. But the impact
of the victory itself was world-wide. In China, in India, in
Africa — throughout the non-Western world — people sat up and
took note. Japan's triumph demonstrated that an Asian nation
could successfully combat the West with its own weapons. The
myth of the white man's invincibility and superiority had been
exploded. The beginning of the end of the white man's domination of the world beyond Europe had dawned.

AFRICA

The first wave of European imperialism, which by the middle of the nineteenth century was changing the direction of Asian history, passed Africa by. One reason for the late development of European interest in Africa lay in its geography: the continent was difficult of access. Few harbors graced its regular shores, and mountain ranges and river cataracts blocked progress from coast to interior. Jungles and tropical diseases underlined the inhospitality of the continent. For almost four centuries after the Portuguese rounded its southern tip and opened the sea route to India and the Far East, Africa remained the "dark continent," so called not after the color of its population but after the degree of Western ignorance of its interior. In the second half of the eighteenth century, adventurous explorations and the profits of the slave trade heightened European interest, but until the 1870's this interest remained primarily commercial, and the few European colonies that nibbled at the coasts were little more than trading posts and ports of call.

The Industrial Revolution gave a new dimension to European

interest in Africa. No longer was Africa merely a supplier of "black ivory" or a steppingstone to the riches of the East; it was a source of raw materials in its own right, a field for investment, and a market for cotton textiles and other manufactures. At the same time the Industrial Revolution provided Europeans with the technical, military, and financial means for conquering the continent, while national rivalries and missionary pressures played their not incompatible parts in bringing Africa within the scope of European imperialism.

In 1870 European holdings in Africa were negligible. The Danes, the first Europeans to forbid the slave trade (1792), had sold out their holdings, and the Dutch were fading out of the picture as a national force. The Portuguese had footholds in Guinea and on some islands in the Gulf of Guinea, as well as more ambitious stretches of land along the lower west and east coasts, but their hold on these regions was tenuous. Spanish claims to Rio de Oro, in the northwest, and to Rio Muni, down the coast, were no more secure. The only possessions of importance, by 1870, were those of the French in the north and of the British in the south.

The French had moved into Algeria, across the Mediterranean, in 1830. Building railways, public utilities, and shipping facilities, they had linked this colony of the north with metropolitan France. To the east, in Egypt, a French company had built the Suez Canal in the late 1860's. In addition to Algeria, and to the influence which control of the canal gave them in Egypt, the French in 1870 held the region of the lower Senegal river in the west, a post further down at Millicouri, a strip of the Ivory Coast along the Gulf of Guinea, and a part of the lower Gabon (or Gabun) river. On the east coast, where the Red Sea narrowed and the Gulf of Aden began, France held the post of Obock; farther south, she had dealings with the northern shores of Madagascar island. But these scattered possessions, even Algeria, were unimpressive. They were not, as yet, conscious steps toward the acquisition of a vast empire.

In 1869, however, when the French took measures to control the finances of the prince of Tunis, who had fallen in arrears in his financial obligations, they launched thereby a period of

French-Italian-British rivalry for influence in this region. As Britain left the field to France in order to smooth ruffled feelings over her own occupation of Cyprus (1878), and as Germany raised no objections, in the hope that an aroused Italy would join Germany and Austria in a Triple Alliance, the French emerged victorious. In 1881, they invaded Tunisia and made it a protectorate. The favorable climate of the area and a relatively enlightened French administration combined to make this a profitable venture, enlisting even the loyalty of many native groups. Farther south, from their scattered posts along the west coast, the French pushed inland in an effort to anticipate rival entrenchment between their possessions in the north and the Congo river. Unable to dislodge the British and the Germans, who meanwhile had entrenched themselves respectively in Nigeria and Kamerun (the Cameroons) — holdings stretching from the Gulf of Guinea to Lake Chad — the French yet succeeded in the late 1890's in creating a huge African empire: it embodied the western Sudan and the Sahara desert, and consisted of French West Africa, French Equatorial Africa, Algeria, and Tunisia, contiguous all.

The British, in 1870, possessed only minor trading posts, scattered along the west coast, at Bathurst, Sierra Leone, the Gold Coast, Lagos, the mouth of the Niger river and Walfish Bay, in addition to their colony in the south. The latter, the former Cape Colony of the Dutch, the British had acquired in the wake of the Napoleonic wars. Rivalry between the Dutch settlers, reinforced by fellow Calvinists from France, on one hand, and the British administrators and settlers, on the other, was a major factor in shaping the history of South Africa. Determined to be free from any outside restraints, Dutch or English, the hardy Calvinist settlers or Boers (peasants) trekked inland. But their harsh treatment of the natives called forth attacks on Europeans throughout the south and of itself invited British intervention. There were other factors too. Aggressive altruism, euphemistically called the "White Man's Burden," the desire for diamonds and gold, and the hunger for land and prestige drew the British after the displaced Dutch, until they annexed their newly founded states, one by one. As with India, there was no master plan of conquest, worked out in London. Local individuals led, almost shoved, a reluctant government on the road to empire; perhaps foremost among these was Cecil Rhodes, an arrogant and eccentric though brilliant businessman and super-patriot, who dreamed not only of a Cape-to-Cairo railway but of English world domination. Step by step the British advanced into Natal, the region between the Orange and Vaal rivers, the Transvaal, and Bechuanaland. Out of the rich tablelands to the north, they carved Rhodesia, and before the end of the century added British Central Africa (later known as Nyasaland) to their empire. As the number of British immigrants increased, so did conflict between Dutch and English settlers. Exasperated, the Boers resorted to arms. For two and a half years (1899–1902) the Boers withstood the British forces. Defeated at last, they were treated generously: the Orange Free State and Transvaal remained within the British empire, but as self-governing colonies, which later joined with Cape Colony and Natal in the Union of South Africa, a dominion like Canada. Nor was the Boer attitude toward the natives — an underlying cause of the war — basically changed. On the contrary, the Dutch view prevailed and the natives were excluded from the government of South Africa.

Meanwhile, British influence had penetrated also North Africa. The Suez Canal, which had been built by the French, soon fell under British control. When Egypt, under its Turkish viceroy, failed to meet its financial obligations, England joined France in assuming control of Egyptian finances. An anti-Western uprising gave an excuse for military action. When the French refused to cooperate with the British, they forfeited their share of control. The British did not make Egypt into a colony, but from then until the first quarter of the twentieth century the British High Commissioner rather than the Turkish viceroy exercised actual power.

From their foothold in Egypt, the British, under Egyptian auspices, penetrated southward into the Sudan, establishing themselves there firmly in 1898, but almost setting off a world war, as the French tried to challenge them at Fashoda. Before this, as noted already, the British had succeeded in extending their holdings along the Niger river. By the end of the century, Nigeria was firmly in their hands.

The organization of the International Association for the Exploration and Colonization of Africa, under the auspices of King Leopold II of Belgium, in 1876, had widened the scope of European competition into a general scramble for spheres of influence. As Belgian, French, English, Portuguese, and German rivalries soon reached the danger point, a conference was held in Berlin (1884–85) to lay down the "rules" for the contest. Except for opposing slavery, the conferees did not consider native interests; the partition of Africa, as of other backward areas, was regarded as the white man's "right." The Congo region, in central Africa, was formed into the Congo Free State, intended as a hunting ground equally open to all. But Leopold managed to make it his exclusive preserve, in which even the activities of his own countrymen were restricted. So oppressive became Leopold's rule that other countries began to intercede on behalf of the natives and to urge reforms. In 1908 the Congo Free State was made into a Belgian colony and provided with a sounder administrative system. Not until after Leopold's death (1909), however, did conditions materially improve.

Germany, a relative latecomer to the colonial race, whose own unification had occurred only in 1871, secured a number of regions scattered across the continent: Togoland and Kamerun in the west, German Southwest Africa down the coast, and German East Africa, adjacent to the Congo Free State. No colonial administration in the late nineteenth century was enlightened, but the Germans were particularly slow in learning to understand the natives.

Italy, another newcomer, whose own unification antedated that of Germany by merely a decade, acquired Eritrea along the Red Sea, and Somaliland farther south. Abyssinia, in between, became for a brief period an Italian protectorate, but regained its independence after the Abyssinians inflicted a humbling defeat on the Italians in 1896 at Adowa.

In 1870 European interest in Africa was primarily commercial. By the end of the century, the continent had been partitioned and parceled out among the colonial powers. Even

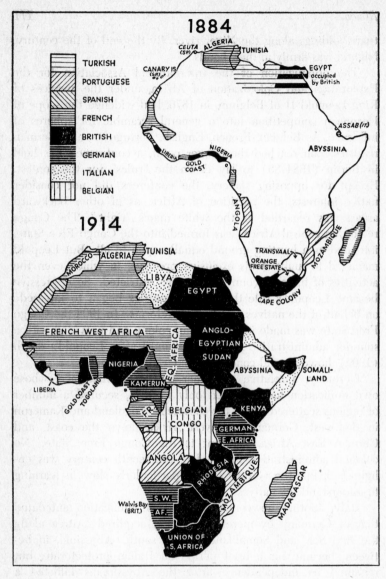

AFRICA IN THE LATE NINETEENTH
AND EARLY TWENTIETH CENTURIES

From R. G. and M. S. Woolbert, "Look at Africa," *Headline Series*
No. 43, Foreign Policy Association, 1943.

the United States of America had become mildly involved, for Liberia, founded in 1822 as a colony for emancipated American slaves, and established as a republic in 1847, remained more or less an American protectorate.

The rapid subjugation of the continent — most of it accomplished within a decade and a half — had taken place with a minimum of fighting, either between rival European powers or with the natives. It was facilitated by the disunity and impotence of the African tribes and by the willingness of many native chieftains to protect and strengthen their position by collaborating with the foreigners.

Professor R. R. Palmer has effectively described the way in which the European yoke was slipped on the Africans:

> Everywhere a variant of the same process was repeated. First, somewhere in the wilderness, would appear a handful of white men, bringing their inevitable treaties — sometimes printed forms. To get what they wanted, the Europeans commonly had to ascribe powers to the chief which by the customs of the tribe he did not possess — powers to convey sovereignty, sell land, or grant mining concessions. Thus the Africans were baffled at the outset by foreign legal conceptions. Then the Europeans would build up the position of the chief, since they themselves had no influence over the people. This led to the widespread system of "indirect rule," by which colonial authorities acted through the existing chiefs and tribal forms. There were many things that only the chief could arrange, such as security for isolated Europeans, porter services, or gangs of workmen to build roads or railroads.
>
> Labor was the overwhelming problem. For pure slavery Europeans now had abhorrence, and they exterminated it wherever they could. But the African, so long as he lived in his own native way, did not react like the free wage-earner postulated in civilized business and economics. He had little sense of individual gain, and almost no use for money. Generally he did not work very hard according to European ideas; work, continuous and laborious work, was in many African societies left to the women. The result was that Europeans all over Africa resorted to forced labor. For road building, systems like the French corvée before the Revolution reappeared. Or the chief would be required to supply a quota of

able-bodied men for a certain length of time, and frequently he did so gladly, to raise his own importance in the eyes of the whites. More indirect methods were also used. The colonial government might levy a hut-tax or a poll-tax, payable only in money, to obtain which the native would have to seek a job. Or the new government, once installed, might allocate so much land to Europeans as private property (another foreign conception) that the local tribe could no longer subsist on the lands that remained to it. Or the whole tribe might be moved to a reservation, like Indians in the United States. In either case, while the women tilled the fields or tended the stock at home, the men would move off to take jobs under the whites for infinitesimal pay. The men then lived in "compounds," away from family and tribal kindred; they became demoralized or even degenerate; and the labor they gave, unintelligent and unwilling, would scarcely have been tolerated in any more civilized community. In these circumstances everything was done to uproot the African, and nothing was done to Westernize him. The old tribal or village society collapsed and nothing replaced it.[1]

In Africa, as in other parts of the world beyond Europe, the Age of Imperialism left a heritage of bitterness and resentment. If the colonies as a whole were raised to higher economic levels, the people as individuals, prior to the belated reforms of the twentieth century, were trampled underfoot. The subjugation of Africa created conditions which in years to come were to threaten the continent, if not the countries of its erstwhile masters, with war and economic chaos.

Epilogue: Part Two

The Age of Imperialism is a chapter in history which most Westerners would now prefer to skip over rather quickly. The "White Man's Burden," the "Mission Civilisatrice," the propa-

[1] R. R. Palmer, *A History of the Modern World,* second edition, revised with the collaboration of Joel Colton (New York: Alfred A. Knopf, Inc., 1956), pp. 639–640.

gation of "Kultur," and other euphemisms for colonialism have a hollow ring today. No American diplomat is likely again to express American policy toward other peoples, as did Ambassador Walter Hines Page, in London, that of the Wilson Administration toward Mexico, in terms of "shooting men into self-government." But the colonial peoples, only recently freed from foreign domination or still under alien rule, continue to linger over every page of that chapter. In part, this may be due to the fact that the smart of defeat outlasts the exhilaration of victory, as in the United States the "War between the States" has been more poignantly remembered in the South than in the North. The preoccupation of the erstwhile and emergent colonial peoples with the Age of Imperialism is, however, not sentimental but dynamic. By arousing antagonism to a common enemy, if only a shadow of his former self, it offers a rallying point for the non-Western peoples, a unity, however ephemeral, for national and international purposes.

The progress of events in China is a case in point. The experience of the Chinese with the early Westerners, in view of China's self-sufficiency and lack of knowledge of the Industrial Revolution in Europe, made the Chinese constraint of Europeans at Canton not unreasonable. But these Chinese restrictions precipitated the English struggle for equality in China, which, ironically, ended in depriving the Chinese of equality vis-à-vis the Westerners. European constraint of the Chinese was in turn to play its part in precipitating China's revolt in our own day and the imposition once again of restrictions on the Westerners. More is involved here than a political seesaw for control. The psychological factors of prestige and equality and purposeful humiliation are of the utmost significance.

In the Age of Imperialism the Western powers won world ascendancy in part because their newly developed industrial strength coincided with the decline and weakness of the old dynasties and the existence of political vacuums in the world beyond Europe. To what extent the accelerating industrialization and the resurgent political self-consciousness of the Asian and African peoples will affect the balance of power in the face of Western disunity and disintegration remains to be seen.

PART THREE

SINCE THE RUSSO-JAPANESE WAR

JAPAN

It was Japan that upset the Western ascendancy with her own brand of imperialism, thereby starting the complex train of events which finally led to the overthrow of European colonialism in Asia, and even, by a kind of chain reaction, in much of Africa. In the early stages of Japan's emergence, however, the Western powers were by no means uniformly hostile to a Japanese counterweight to Russia in the Asian balance. Indeed, in 1904, on the eve of the Russo-Japanese War, Japan had appeared to Americans and Englishmen as the champion of the Open Door policy. Even the Pearl Harbor-like attack on Port Arthur, two days prior to the official declaration of war, aroused little criticism. A British writer in the London *Times* noted merely that "the tremendous and decisive results of success for the national cause are enough to break down all the restraining influences of the code of international and Christian morality." But no sooner had the war ended than Japan followed in the Russian footsteps and began closing the door to Western business in Manchuria and Korea. American attempts to keep the door open and to build an around-the-world transportation system including (or competing with) the Manchurian railways pushed Japan and Russia together in common opposition. In 1907, 1910, and 1916 they concluded treaties of friendship and alliance. In 1907 Japan made the kingdom of Korea into a protectorate, and in 1910 annexed it outright. With the outbreak of World War I, Japan stepped up her continental drive, entered the fray on the side of the Allies, and captured the German possessions in China and in the Pacific Ocean. In 1915 she presented the Chinese government with the infamous Twenty-One Demands, in which she sought not only cession of these former German possessions, but Chinese employment of Japanese as political, military, and financial advisers, Japanese participation in Chinese police administration, and Japanese supply and control of Chinese war materials — in short, domination of China. The storm of indignation which swept through the West, when the Japanese action leaked out, forced Japan to withdraw the more sweeping demands. The remaining demands, though accepted by the Chinese dictator-president, Yüan Shih-k'ai, were repudiated by his successors. But Japan had shown her hand.

In 1917 Japan tried a new approach. In a speech in New York City, Viscount Ishii Kikujiro, Special Envoy to the United States, proclaimed a "Japanese Monroe Doctrine," pledging Japan's defense of Chinese territorial integrity and independence against any aggressor. As the Japanese press put it, "What we want is simply that we become independent of the whites or free yellows of the rampancy of the whites." The Japanese were convinced that it was the destiny of their divinely descended Yamato race to act as champion of the East. "It is incumbent upon the Yamato race," one paper wrote, "to try to recover for the weaker nations of the East their rights, which have been trampled underfoot by other powers." Here were the "Asia for Asians" and "Imperial Way" concepts, which were to chart the course of Japanese imperialism in World War II.

The Communist revolution in Russia (1917) put an end to the budding friendship of Russia and Japan. When the Allied powers, fearful lest vast stores of Allied supplies in Siberia fall into unfriendly hands, called on Japan for assistance in a military intervention, the Japanese participated in the joint expedition. But the Japanese military, ignoring protests of the Western powers and of their own government, sent infinitely more troops than requested and quickly gained control over a large part of Siberia. This put the Japanese in a strong bargaining position at the Paris Peace Conference (1919), where they demanded and received, over Chinese protests, the former German possessions in China and the Pacific. The Japanese withdrew from Siberia only in 1922, probably more because of the increasing burden of the cost of the expedition and the temporary unpopularity of the military within Japan than because of Western opposition.

The First World War had greatly affected Japan internally. Even before the war the political parties had become increasingly vocal in their opposition to the arbitrary sway of the oligarchs, though the party cabinet of Premier Okuma Shigenobu (1914–15) remained under the thumb of the civil and the military oligarchs. The victory of the Allies boosted the prestige of democracy, for it proved the democracies' military strength — a major criterion of Japanese evaluation. Furthermore, during the war Japan, like the United States, had been called upon to furnish the Allies with shipping and supplies, and as a result her industries, like those in the United States, had developed at a remarkable rate. This catapulted the businessman into prominence and, in an era of general prosperity and new respect for democracy, assured him of greater participation in government. At the same time the working class had increased in size, and labor unions assumed political significance. For a decade after World War I, political cabinets ruled Japan. They were far from perfect. They were excessively influenced by special interests and were saddled with corruption. But the fact remains that in the decade after World War I the trend in Japan was toward democratization.

Nor was this trend confined to politics. There was a general loosening of the discipline which had constrained Japanese self-expression since ancient times. The young people strove to be *mobo* (modern boys) and *moga* (modern girls). They dressed in Western fashion, played baseball, danced tangoes, made dates, and generally rebelled against Japanese tradition. There is a definite resemblance here between Japan after World War I and Japan after World War II. The resemblance is the greater because the terrible earthquake of 1923, like the air raids of World War II, leveled most of Yokohama and nearly half of Tokyo, forcing the Japanese to build new and modern cities.

The evil genius which reversed the trend toward democratization in Japan (as in Germany and elsewhere) was the Great Depression. It discredited economic and political *laissez faire*, necessitated government planning and drastic measures. During the period of postwar democratization the conservative and nationalistic elements had not been converted or eliminated, merely overshadowed. Now they came to the fore again, stronger than ever, rejuvenated by young blood and a fantastic mixture of ancient and modern ideology. The militarists of samurai stock still held key positions in the army and navy, but young officers of peasant origin dominated the junior positions. In background and interest the junior officers were closely identified with the rural population (the majority of the Japanese) and its needs; they were hostile to capitalism, the bourgeoisie, and urban life in general. In the 1930's they emerged as the standard bearers of a radical nationalism, which envisaged a socialist state run by the military under the continued reign of the emperor.

Japan's industrialization had brought with it a great increase in population. By the time of the depression, when protective tariff barriers sprang up abroad, Japan could no longer sustain her teeming population with her own agricultural resources. The militarists had favored continental expansion all along; it was a relatively simple matter now to persuade the other Japanese that the acquisition of new territories was essential to the economic survival of their country. Most needed were raw materials and markets for Japan's industries, sources of additional agricultural produce, and *Lebensraum*. The financial oligarchy put up little

THE JAPANESE EMPIRE IN 1933

From Meribeth E. Cameron, Thomas H. D. Mahoney and George E. McReynolds, *China, Japan and the Powers;* copyright 1952 The Ronald Press Company.

opposition. Business profited from territorial expansion, and there was little temptation to run the risk of assassination at the hand of the Japanese militarists.

Two major developments characterized the 1930's. The first was the mushrooming of chauvinistic associations of various sorts, ranging from the Young Men's Association and the Imperial League of Young Officers to the secret and fanatical Black Dragon (actually Amur River) Society. The other major development was the increasing violence and independence of action of the military. In 1931 the military attacked Manchuria without governmental sanction, and later that year, with the support of the ultra-nationalistic organizations, made two vain attempts to establish a military dictatorship in Japan. Other attempts followed; though also unsuccessful, these resulted in the murder of leading statesmen and politicians and in the intimidation of many more. The hesitancy of the courts of law to punish the assassins severely, on the ground that they had acted from genuinely patriotic motives, and the inability of Parliament to withhold funds from the military, left the latter without restraint. Further inflamed by the writings of General Araki Sadao, who inveighed equally against capitalism and communism and provided philosophical, religious, and economic arguments for Japanese expansion, the ardor of the military extremists was by 1936 near the danger point. This does not mean that the average Japanese wanted war. On the contrary: the election results of 1936 registered a protest against militarism. Yet this very protest prompted the militarists to attempt another coup d'état. Once again leading Japanese statesmen were murdered. But the coup failed. No military dictatorship was established.

The full-scale invasion of China in 1937, however, silenced most moderates and liberals, or left them impotent. In 1938 the government was voted direct control over all material and human resources in case of emergency. By 1940 all political parties had been dissolved by the state, and the Imperial Rule Assistance Association organized in their stead. This was not a political party, but an agency through which the government could enlist the support of its members while giving them the illusion of political participation. No single dictator emerged as the head of the state, as in Germany. Even General Tojo Hideki, who had almost dictatorial powers during the war, did not rule the country single-handed. In line with Japanese tradition, an oligarchy wielded power behind the scenes.

Japanese expansion into China brought Japan into conflict with the same powers that had favored if not supported her in her struggle with Russia in 1904. This was not surprising, for the issue was the same — the Open Door in China — except that Japan was now the one to exclude Western business. The League of Nations censured the Kwantung Army's thrust into Manchuria (1931) and the subsequent establishment of the puppet state of Manchukuo, but Japan merely withdrew from the League. The United States refused to recognize Manchukuo, and relations between Japan and the United States, strained already because of America's exclusion policy in immigration, continued to deteriorate. But these were years of world-wide depression, and the Western powers were too much preoccupied with internal problems to interfere more actively. The acceleration of Japanese expansion in 1937 and the bombing of the American gunboat *Panay* on the Yangtze river aroused increasing American opposition and a determination to resort to measures "short of war." In 1939 the United States gave notice of the termination, in January, 1940, of her commercial treaty with Japan; prepared to enforce an embargo on the shipment of scrap iron and high-octane gasoline to Japan; and granted loans to China. Japanese designs on the Dutch East Indies and French Indo-China, as war broke out in Europe, similarly met with American disapproval. It became evident that the United States in seeking to preserve the status quo in the Far East was the major obstacle to Japan's dream of great conquests.

The Japanese campaign in China was at once both successful and unsuccessful. It was successful in that the Japanese overran the most desirable parts of China, occupying her great cities and harbors and industrial centers. It was unsuccessful in that the Chinese government refused to surrender, and stubbornly continued the war. The Japanese became involved ever more deeply, and the seemingly endless struggle began to weigh heavily on Japanese morale and resources. The American decision to withhold fuel from the Japanese war machine was a serious deprivation, and the Japanese, unwilling to forfeit their hard-won conquests, turned to the Dutch East Indies and French Indo-China for the raw materials they needed. But China remained the primary objective. In the American-Japanese negotiations of 1941 Japan appeared willing to bargain on most points, but was adamant on one: she would not (and for domestic political reasons could not) pull out from China as the United States demanded. Sooner or later a clash with the United States seemed inevitable. As American aid to China increased and the United States began to rearm, Japan decided to strike while there was still a chance of success.

For years various political observers had predicted a conflict between Japan and the Soviet Union, and as the Nazi invasion of Russia bogged down, Germany would have welcomed a second front in the east. But Japan decided otherwise. Siberia was less attractive than Southeast Asia in climate and resources, the Soviet armies had given a worthy account of themselves during border clashes in the 1930's, and a campaign in the Pacific would permit the fuller utilization of Japanese naval as well as military might.

Japan's decision to go to war with the United States was not taken lightly. Leading naval officers objected. Even the army did not hope for total victory, but calculated that the United States, with her Pacific fleet shattered in a surprise attack, would be willing to come to terms. It was a calculated risk based on a crucial misunderstanding of American psychology; far from disheartening the American people, the attack on Pearl Harbor on December 7, 1941, in advance of a declaration of war, united them in angry determination to crush Japan.

In the early stages of the war the Japanese were remarkably successful. Their armies flowed into Southeast Asia and the Pacific islands and threatened to inundate most of the world beyond Europe. But the United States, marshaling tremendous resources, was able to outproduce and outfight Japan and finally to threaten her with literal oblivion if she did not surrender unconditionally.

The total destruction of Japan's ability to wage war again was justified in view of Japan's record of aggression, but it failed to take into account the need to preserve the balance of power in the Far East. As later events were to prove, China was not strong enough to step into Japan's role of counterweight to

Russia, and Japan's impotence would create a political vacuum into which the Soviet Union would not unwillingly be drawn. Once again, as in 1904, Russian and Western interests were to clash, but this time there would be no Japanese army or navy to champion the Open Door — the antithesis of the Iron Curtain.

The unconditional surrender of Japan was attained with unexpected ease. As late as February, 1945 (before the explosion of the first atom bomb), the combined Anglo-American Chiefs of Staff had estimated that Japan proper would have to be invaded at great cost in American lives, and that even with Russian help it would require eighteen months after the defeat of Germany to bring Japan to her knees. The suddenness of the Japanese surrender and the unhindered occupation of the home islands owed much to the personal intervention of Emperor Showa (Hirohito). Traditionally the emperor acted only on the advice of his ministers, and in 1941 the ministers were unanimous in their recommendation to go to war with the United States. Thus, whatever his own feelings may have been, the emperor had little opportunity to express them. In 1945 his ministers were divided whether to surrender or go down fighting, and he was in a position to lend his weight to the cause of peace. The emperor's command that all resistance cease was obeyed, and the Pacific war ended as dramatically as it had begun.

The occupation which followed was predominantly American. Japan was not divided among the occupying countries, but was governed by one Supreme Command of the Allied Powers, which included Allied representatives. The Supreme Commander, General Douglas MacArthur, and the bulk of the occupation forces were American.

The original purpose of the occupation was to disarm Japan and to deprive her of the ability ever to wage aggressive war again. It was not the purpose, at first, to democratize Japan but merely to free her of the military strait jacket and to withdraw once she had chosen a responsible government. Gradually, however, democratization became a definite objective, and every effort was made to imbue the Japanese with an appreciation of democratic ideals and practices.

The impact of the occupation on Japanese life cannot be exaggerated. The Japanese had always been eager students of foreign ways. But never before had so many Japanese been exposed directly to Westerners at length; never before had they been encouraged so persistently and persuasively to adopt new ideas. To many Westerners, Japanese emulation of democracy and Japanese smiles were a sham. But the Japanese were genuinely impressed with the strength and success of the Allied democracies and were sincerely eager to make the best of a bad situation and to profit from their compulsory education.

Democracy is a way of life. It cannot be imposed by military decree. There is no way of telling how permanent the reforms implanted by the occupation authorities will be. Perhaps the greatest contribution of the occupation was the drafting of a new constitution. The emperor was permitted to remain at the head of the state, but he was shorn of his divinity and autocratic authority. The constitution is one of the most democratic in the world, guaranteeing the people's right to "life, liberty, and the pursuit of happiness" and equality under the law without discrimination "in political, economic or social relations, because of race, creed, sex, social status, or family origin." It enumerates such rights as universal suffrage, secrecy of ballot, freedom of thought, conscience and speech, marriage based on the mutual consent of both parties, academic freedom, the right to maintain the minimum standards of wholesome and cultured living, and the right of collective bargaining. To be sure, the constitution is a piece of paper and of itself does not guarantee that the Japanese will adhere to its provisions. It does not make impossible a return to the autocratic ways of old. Its great significance lies in the fact that it has removed the obstacles to democracy that were inherent in the old constitution. If the people of Japan choose to retain the democratic way of life, it is now constitutionally possible for them to do so.

The outbreak of the Cold War showed that World War II, like World War I, had failed to create a world in which armies were no longer necessary. The occupation did not abandon the objective of democracy, but it now reversed the policy of economic decentralization and demilitarization. Ironically, the Japanese had learned their lesson all too well, and were reluctant to heed American urging that the constitution be amended to permit the rebuilding of the armed forces.

In 1951 the United States and most of the Allies (with the notable exception of the Soviet Union and China) concluded a peace treaty with Japan, whereby the Japanese empire was reduced to the four main islands. Under a separate agreement American security forces were permitted to remain temporarily, but Japan had regained her independence in theory, and step by step began to assert her independence in fact. In 1956 Japan was admitted to the United Nations. At the polls and in foreign policy the Japanese people showed that they were ready again to shape their own destiny.

KOREA

Japan had fought two wars to free Korea from Chinese and Russian influence. In 1910 she made Korea into a colony of her own — not an improvement for the inhabitants, since Japanese colonial administration was unenlightened. The Japanese have pointed with pride to the modernization of Korea, but the benefits of this modernization reverted primarily to Japan. The Koreans were excluded from the economic as well as the political and administrative management of their country; Japanese were given preference in education, in employment, and quite generally in most fields of endeavor. Unlike the British, French, and Dutch, who interfered relatively little with the indigenous ways of life in their colonies, the Japanese, themselves related racially and culturally to the Koreans, made every effort to Japanize them. In this respect Japanese policy in Korea was more akin to Russian policy in Poland. Native nationalism was ruthlessly silenced by the Japanese, and advocates of independence had to seek refuge abroad — in the United States, China, and Russia.

In the 1940's the prospects of Japanese defeat had reawakened Korean aspirations for independence, but a generation of Japanese rule had left Korea without the necessary experience for self-government. The victorious Allies deemed it necessary, therefore, to provide for a transition period of not more than five years during which Korea, though independent, would be under the trusteeship of the United States, Russia, Great Britain, and China.

Meanwhile the surrender of Japanese forces in Korea had to be accepted, and American and Russian troops poured into Korea. For purposes of military convenience the operations of these troops had been separated by the thirty-eighth parallel, but as relations between the United States and Russia changed from amity to hostility, the temporary division of Korea into zones was solidified. Attempts to reunify the country under a national administration failed, as the United States refused to go along with Soviet insistence that only parties which had accepted the Communist point of view should be consulted in the formation of a provisional government.

The American and Russian zones made unequal progress. Less inclined to drastic measures, hesitant to impose their will, and short of Korean-speaking personnel, the Americans in the south retained Japanese administrators for several months, then leaned on Koreans who spoke English, that is, on Koreans who happened to be members of the conservative upper class. Believing in political freedom, the Americans permitted the establishment of any number of political parties, which, owing to political inexperience and a tradition of violence, fostered unrest rather than responsible government. The Russians in North Korea acted with greater determination and less scruple. Only one party, the Communist New People's Party, was permitted, and the administration of the Russian zone was surrendered almost immediately to the party leaders, who could readily be manipulated.

In 1948 administrative authority in South Korea was transferred to the government of the Republic of Korea, duly elected under the supervision of the United Nations. The Russian zone

KOREA IN 1951

From Meribeth E. Cameron, Thomas H. D. Mahoney and George E.
McReynolds, *China, Japan and the Powers;* copyright 1952 The
Ronald Press Company.

remained apart, access having been denied to the United Nations
supervisory commission. The constitution of the new Republic
of Korea provided for a legislative assembly and a strong presi-

dent, elected by the assembly. No limit was set on the number of four-year terms a president could serve, and Dr. Syngman Rhee, the first president, continued in office for many years. The Republic of Korea encompassed actually only the region south of the thirty-eighth parallel. Its constitution embodied, however, the whole peninsula and hopefully left the door open for eventual unification. But in the north a rival "permanent" government had been set up: the Communist-controlled Korean People's Republic. With less than ten million inhabitants in 1949, North Korea was only half as populous as South Korea, yet had a much stronger military machine. When Russia unilaterally withdrew her forces in 1949, thereby bringing pressure on the United States soon to do likewise, North Korea remained in a favorable position. So vociferous was Syngman Rhee in his promises to reunify Korea, that the United States feared he might invade the north, and hesitated to build up the military might of the southern Republic.

When the North Korean forces struck across the thirty-eighth parallel in June, 1950, South Korea was unable to hold its own, and a United Nations expeditionary force had to be dispatched to roll back the aggressor. The opportunity now presented itself to reunify Korea under the auspices of the United Nations, but before unification could be accomplished Communist Chinese "volunteers" intervened on the side of North Korea. A stalemate developed (partly because the United States chose not to strike directly at Chinese bases beyond Korea lest a general war be precipitated), and after lengthy armistice negotiations the status quo ante bellum was restored. But the ultimate unification of Korea, by force if need be, remained in the minds of Korean leaders north and south.

INDIA AND PAKISTAN

The year 1905 saw a stiffening of Indian resistance to British rule. The nationalistic fever had been heightened by developments abroad. The formidable resistance of colonials in Abyssinia and South Africa to European armed might was encouraging, and the defeat of the proud Russian empire by the Japanese left little doubt in Asian minds that a new era had dawned. Moderate spokesmen in the Indian National Congress now began to advocate the attainment of self-government by constitutional means, while more extreme nationalists, dominantly in Bengal, prepared to use force. Guided by the methods of revolutionaries in Italy, Ireland, and Russia, and aided by expert European advice on bomb-making, the Indian extremists commenced their sporadic terrorist attacks in 1906. Indian agitation and the accession of a Liberal government in England combined to bring about a modification of British rule in 1909, but the extension of representative government was very limited, and the British retained virtually complete control. In 1911 the capital of India was moved from Calcutta to New Delhi and the partition of Bengal was revoked (concessions to Moslem and Hindu sentiment, respectively), but there were no major changes in colonial rule. Yet the Indian independence movement remained primarily moderate, for most of the intellectual leaders, because of their British education, were steeped in the traditions and values of English liberalism.

The weakness of the Indian independence movement did not lie in its moderation. It stemmed partly from conflicts of interest within its own midst, notably between the Hindu majority and the Moslem minority. The proportionate representatation sought by the Hindus, for example, threatened to freeze the Moslems in a position of political insignificance; on the other hand, the communal representation desired by the Moslems would give them exaggerated political importance at the expense of the Hindus. But the major source of the independence movement's weakness prior to 1914 was the narrowness of its base. It was built essentially on the Western-educated middle class, whose members, like their political counterparts in early-nineteenth-century England, ignored the economic needs of the lower classes in their preoccupation with political rights for themselves. All this changed with the advent of World War I.

India did not take advantage of large-scale British troop withdrawals to throw off English rule. Several German-inspired plots were contrived, but they were insignificant in comparison with the remarkable loyalty of the country as a whole to Great Britain and its generous support in men and funds of the British war effort. Nonetheless Indian nationalism received a tremendous boost. There were a number of reasons for this. The British offended many Indian intellectuals by failing to make full use of their proffered services; the length and mounting costs and hardships of the war fostered discontent; there was the example of the Irish revolt of 1916. But the greatest factor in the growth of nationalism was the crusading spirit with which many of the Allies had become imbued during the war, the war which was to make the world safe for democracy, with national self-determination one of the coveted goals. In 1916 three developments advanced the national cause: a Home Rule League was founded; a number of members of the imperial legislative council petitioned the government for a more nearly equal status for India; the Indian National Congress (a predominantly Hindu body, in which the extremists had gained the ascendance) and the Moslem League joined in supporting home rule for India, a rapprochement brought about in part by Moslem resentment over Britain's war with the Ottoman Empire, whose head was the spiritual leader of Moslems everywhere. In 1917, in response to pressure within the British Parliament itself as well as to Indian demands, the British government formally proclaimed as its goal in India "the progressive realization of responsible government as an integral part of the British Empire." In 1919 modifications in the government of India abolished the British majority in the Delhi legislature and gave Indian ministers full control of some departments, but the British, through the emergency powers of the governor-general, still retained effective control. When the war ended, demands increased among Indian leaders that Great Britain repay India for her loyalty by granting her home rule.

The great illusion of a better world to emerge from the war had gripped the people of India, as of Europe. Not merely the intellectuals but people of all classes were filled with great expectations. The failure of these expectations to materalize, indeed the deterioration of living conditions in the wake of a dreadful influenza epidemic (1918–19), led to the same great postwar disillusionment in India as in Europe. In Italy the popular unrest was galvanized by Benito Mussolini; in India it was marshaled with equal effect but greater humanity by Mohandas K. Gandhi (the Mahatma or Saint), whose ascetic piety, simplicity, quiet dignity, and trust in nonviolence contrasted sharply with the strutting bravado of European nationalism.

The passive resistance of Gandhi's adherents deprived the British of the cooperation which their plans for the gradual transfer of power required. Unwilling to withdraw forthwith, unable to gain the necessary cooperation, the British were faced with repeated crises. Thus the India Act of 1919, which provided India with a dyarchy of bureaucratic and responsible government (leaving the administration of such key departments as justice, police, and irrigation under British control but putting local government, education, agriculture, and the like into Indian hands), though it was a major step toward self-government and met with the approval of moderates in India and in England, was opposed by Gandhi, as would have been any other provision short of complete self-government. To say that all of Gandhi's actions were motivated purely by his sense of morality would be to do injustice to his political astuteness, but it must be realized that Gandhi's opposition (again perhaps not only for moral reasons) was not to British rule alone, but to Western, if not modern, civilization in general. The good life, he believed, was the simple agrarian life, and the boycott he led extended to Western manufactures as well as to governmental affairs. His simple garment and spinning wheel became the symbol of political and economic independence and of the moral life.

Addressing himself at first to the upper classes, Gandhi enjoined them from participating in governmental service and from sending their sons to college for education in Western ways. Gradually he increased his audience, and in 1922 launched a campaign of massive civil disobedience. But his pleas for nonviolence went unheeded. Temporarily, therefore, he called off the campaign of massive civil disobedience and of noncooperation, shocked by the cost in human lives and influenced perhaps by the fear of his middle-class colleagues in the National Congress that a mass movement might encourage opposition to all law and property, including Indian. Shortly afterwards Gandhi was arrested and imprisoned for two years, but the national consciousness of Indians of all classes had been awakened. Young Hindu nationalists of a more radical bent came to the fore, and under the leadership of Jawaharlal Nehru, an English-educated Brahman of wealthy family, pressed for economic and social as well as political reforms. At the same time, however, nationalism deepened the division between Hindus and Moslems. Guided by Mohammed Ali Jinnah, a well-to-do lawyer, also educated in England, the Moslems began to clamor for a state of their own.

In 1929 Great Britain stated its determination to lead India to dominion status, and projected a series of conferences in London, at which English and Indian leaders could join in working out the necessary framework of government. Six years later, after continued unrest in India and heated debate in England, Parliament's Government of India Act of 1935 set forth the new constitution. It provided for a federal union of British India and the princely states; the old dyarchy of responsibilities was to continue only on the federal level, while the provinces received autonomy in local government. It provided for a bicameral legislature, with the electorate divided into several groups (Moslems, Sikhs, Christians, Europeans, Labor, General Population, and so forth). But the British still controlled more than just defense and foreign relations; they retained "safeguards" of importance. The constitution thus fell short of dominion status and was rejected by the National Congress party. Nor was federation automatic, and the princely states, partly for fear of radical reform sentiment, refused to join. The Moslem League too, feeling increasingly discriminated against by the dominant National Congress party, came out in opposition to the Act of 1935, and demanded autonomy for its coreligionists. Only on the provincial level were the new reforms instituted, therefore, though with considerable success.

When World War II broke out in 1939, the British Parliament granted complete emergency powers over the provinces to the viceroy and central government of India, the viceroy declared war on Germany, and the stage was set for renewed pressure for complete and immediate independence. The National Congress party boycotted the war effort and demanded the calling of an Indian constitutional convention, while the Moslem League, unable to get from the Congress party the guarantees it required, worked for independence from both Great Britain and the Congress party. But as England's position in Europe became critical and India herself was threatened by Japanese invasion, the Indian war effort swung into higher gear despite Gandhi's opposition.

In 1942 the eminent British statesman Sir Stafford Cripps hastened to India with a declaration specifying the steps England would take after the war to give India full and equal dominion status, providing even for the independence of those states which chose not to join the Indian Union, as well as for the secession of the Union as a whole from the British Commonwealth. But the Cripps proposals were turned down, as much because of mutual distrust among different religious and cultural factions within India as because of Indian impatience with further delays. The National Congress party, for example, objected particularly that the constitution envisaged by Cripps permitted the partition of India, while the Moslem League objected that it did not stipulate for partition clearly enough. As Gandhi, Nehru, and other Congress leaders endangered the war effort by campaigning for the exodus of the British and their Allies, they were incarcerated. This gave the Moslem League the opportunity to strengthen its position. British attempts to come to terms with Indian leaders in the summer of 1945 continued to be unsuccessful, primarily because what was acceptable to the National Congress party was unacceptable to the Moslem League and vice versa.

With the return to power of the Labor party in England in the autumn of 1945, steps were taken at last for the calling of elections in India, preparatory to the promised constitutional convention. Anti-British and anti-Western demonstrations continued as nationalism grew, but the advice and help of a group of English cabinet members who arrived in February, 1946, were not spurned by the Indian leaders. As before, the major conflict was between the National Congress party and the Moslem League, the former wanting a strong central government, the latter a decentralized federal system. A compromise plan, carefully prepared by the cabinet mission with a view to maintaining Indian unity while safeguarding Moslem interests, failed to overcome the Hindu-Moslem schism. Riots broke out in various places and threatened to flare into civil war. Without choice, the British government announced in June, 1947, through Lord Louis Mountbatten, the new viceroy, that within a matter

of months it would surrender its governmental authority to two
governments, the Union of India and Pakistan, each with
dominion status. The following month the Indian Independence
Bill was enacted by the British Parliament, and on August 15,
1947, Pakistan and the Union of India attained their independence, all but three of the princely states — Junagadh, Kashmir, and Hyderabad — having joined with one or the other.
(Eventually Junagadh joined Pakistan; the other two, India.)
So bitter was the heritage of Hindu-Moslem rivalry and dis-
agreement over the proper disposition of these three states,
especially Kashmir, that incidents and riots continued to plague
the two nations, and for a year or so they barely skirted full-
scale war. It was Gandhi's effort to halt the persecution of
Moslems in India that led to his assassination in January, 1948,
by a Hindu extremist. But his death was not in vain. It shocked
Hindus and Moslems alike into a cessation of strife, permitting
the governments of India and Pakistan to turn their energies
to the constitutional tasks at hand.

The Constitution of 1950 (amended in 1951 and 1953) made
the Union of India [1] a democratic republic — a federation of
states with a strong central government, after the American pattern, within the Commonwealth of Nations. It vested legislative
power in a parliament of two chambers, upper and lower: the
Council of States and the House of the People. Executive
authority was placed in the hands of a president, a prime minister, and a cabinet responsible to the lower house. The constitution guaranteed the usual democratic rights and outlawed the
caste system. Beyond that, it held forth as a guide for legislation
such social and economic principles as fair distribution of wealth,
decent working conditions, equal pay for men and women, and
free education. With an area of a million and a quarter square
miles and the second largest population of any country on the
globe — a population approaching 400,000,000 — India constituted the largest democracy in the world.

The problems the new republic faced were many. The young
revolutionaries who had led the way to independence were

[1] Or Bharat, as the state was called in Hindi, the official national language.

old men now. Younger men had yet to be trained up as competent successors. India's entry on the stage of world affairs occurred just when the abilities of the most experienced diplomats and statesmen everywhere were taxed to the utmost by the sudden intensification of the bitter ideological conflict between Communism and Democracy. Confronted with overwhelming problems at home, Nehru as Prime Minister refused to side with the democracies, whose forces included the imperialist powers of old, or with the Communists, whose economic blueprints failed to disguise a new imperialism. In a world that took the attitude, "You're for us or against us," the neutralism of Nehru's India reaped jeers from both camps.

The most crucial problems were economic. India was a country with a woefully low standard of living, a country ridden by poverty, disease, superstition, and ignorance. The insufficient food supply was steadily outstripped by the ever-multiplying population: reverence for the cow and opposition to birth control were but two of the better-known examples of the hurdles the government faced. Large-scale long-range planning was necessary, and Nehru initiated a series of five year plans to develop the agricultural and industrial production of the country. Shunning the easy street of totalitarian methods, the government sent thousands of trained workers to villages to teach the people how to raise their productiveness and their standard of living through communal projects.

As if the enormous tasks confronting India internally were not enough, the frantic "leap forward" to industrialization of her Communist neighbor, China, has involved her in a race that pits democratic against totalitarian methods of economic development. India's hope of heading a "third force" of neutralist nations, effective in counteracting or modifying the struggle between "East" and "West," has had limited results so far, but on the relative measure of her success in raising the standard of living of her masses by democratic means may depend the future political allegiance of her own people and of the other underdeveloped and "uncommitted" nations of the world beyond Europe. Thus it is possible that India holds the ultimate bal-

INDIA AND PAKISTAN

ance of power between Democracy and Communism everywhere.

The new nation of Pakistan, which came into being in 1947, was composed of the predominantly Moslem states. Since these were not contiguous, Pakistan was divided into two parts — Western and Eastern Pakistan, with the bulk of India in between. Small in comparison with India, Pakistan was the fifth most populous state in the world, housing in its 360,000 square miles a population of over 75,000,000. Unlike the Republic of India, which inherited much of the British administrative system, Pakistan had to start almost from scratch, with a new capital in the west, at Karachi, and a meager body of civil servants. For this reason the new republic, which chose also to remain within the Commonwealth, continued to rely heavily on the services of English officers and administrators. Following the death of her founder, Mohammed Ali Jinnah, in the fall of 1948, Pakistan was guided by Liaquat Ali Khan and a galaxy of other statesmen, most of them Oxford-educated, who had to devote a large part of their time and energy to holding together the various peoples of the federation, since religion was usually the only common bond. Conflict over representation and political power was especially pronounced between Western and Eastern Pakistan, the latter a fraction of the former in size but with a larger population.

Administered temporarily according to the basic framework of the Government of India Act of 1935, Pakistan struggled laboriously to draw up a constitution of its own. At last, in the spring of 1956, a constitution was adopted, and Pakistan was transformed into an Islamic republic, a federation, with a one-chamber legislature and a parliamentary form of government embodying many British and American features. The constitution guaranteed the usual civil rights and, like the Indian constitution, spoke of economic and social legislation on behalf of the people. But though Pakistan made remarkable strides economically and took a forthright stand on the side of the American-supported South East Asia Treaty Organization, she continued to experience far greater internal political difficulties than India. More than once constitutional government was temporarily abrogated, and Pakistan still is further away from democratic government than India. But democratization is a slow and difficult process, not amenable to dictate. For the time being, Pakistan has not abandoned democracy as the ultimate goal, and her progress, if compared with countries of the same level of limited political experience, holds forth hope of brighter days ahead. In October, 1959, Pakistan began moving the capital from Karachi to Rawalpindi, seven hundred and fifty miles northward, to get the seat of government away from the mounting business influence.

SOUTHEAST ASIA

The twentieth century brought great changes to Southeast Asia. In the years following the Russo-Japanese War and World War I, nationalistic feeling became increasingly vocal. It was greatly intensified in the 1920's, and with the Japanese conquests of 1941 and after, reached full fruition. To be sure, the Japanese substituted their own imperialism for that of the West, but in the process they exploded the myth of the white man's superiority. In a sense they had done so already in 1904–05, but now they humiliated the Westerner right in front of the average man in Southeast Asia. They mounted a far-reaching propaganda campaign and, as the fortunes of war reversed and the West prepared to strike back, proclaimed the independence of some of the colonial states. At the same time, the Japanese occupation made greater use of native talent in the administration of the colonies, and in its final stages trained native troops and officers to withstand the Allied forces. And while the Japanese thus provided nationalist leaders and forces with needed experience, the Communists gained practice and influence in the guerrilla resistance to the Japanese.

Thus, though Allied victory shattered Japanese imperialism in Southeast Asia, Japan's temporary conquest precipitated the later loss of colonies there by the Western powers. When Japan surrendered, most of Southeast Asia was still in Japanese hands. Before the colonial powers could resume their old position, native leaders took control and proclaimed the independence of their lands. Attempts by the Dutch and French to gain their former position only showed that it was impossible to return to pre-war colonialism. A new era had dawned for Southeast Asia.

In the Philippines ultimate independence had been promised by the Americans from the very beginning. An elective assembly was provided by the Organic Act of 1902, and Filipinos shared in the government of the islands. The Philippines' closest tie with the United States was an economic one. The United States did not there practice the Open Door she preached elsewhere, and the preferential status of American businessmen, together with the absence of tariff barriers, channeled most Philippine trade to the United States. With the depression, producers within the United States began to clamor for protection against Philippine competition, and the old advocates of Philippine independence received new support in Washington. The Tydings-McDuffie Act of 1934 authorized a constitutional convention, and in 1935 the Philippines received a commonwealth government. The economy needed a period of gradual readjustment, however, and full independence was postponed for a decade. Japanese expansion added a strategic angle to American interests, but the United States remained true to its promise. When the Japanese, who had overrun the islands during World War II, were driven out again, constitutional government was resumed promptly without any interlude of military rule. On July 4, 1946, the independent Republic of the Philippines was officially inaugurated. The government, under the constitution of 1935, as amended in 1940, continued to be a democracy with a strong president and a bicameral legislature.

The Philippine republic experienced political conflicts and growing pains, but remained democratic and relatively friendly

to the United States. The only Christian nation in Southeast
Asia, it became an active member of the United Nations and of
the South East Asia Treaty Organization, taking an unequivocal
stand against Communism at home and abroad.

In the Dutch East Indies the absolute authority of the government of Holland was relaxed in the 1920's, and the partly
native Indonesian People's Council received co-legislative powers
with the governor-general in 1927. Virulent nationalism, directed
against the economically dominant Chinese as well as against
the Dutch, was suppressed, however, as was Communism. The
Japanese conquest of the Dutch East Indies advanced native
nationalism to such an extent that the postwar willingness of
the Dutch to meet the prewar demands for greater autonomy
was no longer adequate. The nationalists had proclaimed an
independent Indonesian Republic as soon as the war ended,
before the Allies had returned to receive the surrender of the
Japanese, and Republican forces took effective control of most
of Java, Madura, and Sumatra. The rest of the Indies reverted
to Dutch administration. After four years of repeated negotiations, punctuated both by intermittent 'warfare and by moral
pressure from the United Nations, agreement was reached on a
United States of Indonesia connected with the Netherlands. But
by August, 1950, the United States of Indonesia had merged
into the Republic of Indonesia (the largest and most influential
of the member states), and within half a decade the Indone-
sians officially separated from the Netherlands.

Embracing all of what had once been the Dutch East Indies, except Western New Guinea at the eastern end of the
archipelago, the Republic of Indonesia covered an area of over
735,000 square miles or more than sixty times the area of the
Netherlands. Its population (in 1957) of over 85,000,000 was almost twice that of France. Indonesia had a president and a
unicameral legislature, but experimented more with "guided
democracy" than true popular participation. An authoritarian
tradition, public inexperience in self-government, and postwar
brigandage contributed to this trend. As economic conditions
continued to deteriorate and the country seethed with rebellion,

the temptation beckoned to restore order by military dictatorship.

French Indo-China consisted of a colony, Cochin China, and four protectorates, Annam, Cambodia, Laos, and Tongking. Slightly larger in size than France herself, Indo-China was rich in raw materials (zinc ore, rubber, coal, tin, copra) and food products (rice, cinnamon, pepper, tea). Strategically it was a springboard for French interests in China, notably in Yünnan province and on Hainan island. In the protectorates a certain amount of local authority was retained and native customs were left relatively untouched, and yet government rested securely in the hands of the governor-general in Hanoi. After the fall of France, the Japanese obtained from the Vichy government in 1940 the right to pass through Indo-China and make use of bases there; by the time they unleashed the Pacific phase of World War II the following year, the Japanese were in actual control of the colony. French impotence shattered French prestige permanently.

In Indo-China as elsewhere, anticolonialism and nationalism had once before, in 1905, been encouraged by Japanese exposure of Western weakness. In Indo-China as elsewhere, Western education, however limited, had fostered nationalistic and revolutionary ideals. But nationalism was slow to develop in Indo-China before World War II, hindered as it was by diversity in the native population — the Annamites were as hostile to the Chinese, the Cambodians, and the inhabitants of Laos as to the French — and by conflict in political aims. On the eve of their own defeat, the Japanese proclaimed Emperor Bao Dai of Annam ruler of Indo-China. He was not able to retain his position beyond the Japanese surrender, however, and a nationalist government headed by Ho Chi Minh, an old revolutionary leader with Communist ties, came to power and proclaimed the independence of Indo-China in the form of the Republic of Viet Nam. Meanwhile the French in their constitution of the Fourth Republic provided for a federation of the Indo-Chinese states within the "French Union," an association of autonomous states somewhat on the Commonwealth pattern, but with more central

control and hence less viability than the (British) Commonwealth of Nations. The adherents of the Republic of Viet Nam
insisted on a greater degree of independence, and fighting ensued. The French succeeded in reconquering Cochin China,
Cambodia, and Laos, and put forth the Annamite government
of Cochin China as a rival to the government of Ho Chi Minh.
But they were unable to regain Annam and Tongking. They set
up the "Provisional" Central Government of Viet Nam with
Bao Dai as head, claiming it had authority over Annam and
Tongking as well as Cochin China. Cambodia and Laos were
declared independent but "associated" states within the French
Union.

There now were two governments of Viet Nam. The original Republic of Viet Nam (or Democratic Republic of Viet
Nam, as it came to be known) received in popular appellation
the name Viet Minh, because it was in the hands of the Viet
Minh party. Situated in the north, adjacent to China, it was
also referred to as North Viet Nam in distinction to South
Viet Nam, the French-backed section. The victory of the Communists in China insured the Communist-dominated government
in North Viet Nam of outside support and permitted the
continuation of the war with the French on an increased scale.
With the government in the north recognized by the Soviet
Union and Communist China, and the government in the south
by the United States and her allies, the colonial struggle in
Indo-China became enmeshed in the global conflict between
the Communist world and the Western democracies. At the
Geneva Conference of 1954, which dealt primarily with the
Korean problem, the dividing line between North and South
Viet Nam was drawn roughly across the seventeenth parallel.

In 1955 Bao Dai, who had the unfortunate reputation of
playboy, was succeeded by the far more competent nationalist
leader Ngo Dinh Diem, who was able with American economic
aid to re-establish a certain stability in South Viet Nam. Cambodia and Laos too received American assistance and thereby
were enabled at last to stand independent of France.

In Siam (known since 1939, with but a brief interlude, as

Thailand) nationalism had grown apace too, with the added touch of pride that Siam alone among her neighbors had withstood European conquest. In 1932 a coup d'état had terminated the absolute rule of old, and a constitutional monarchy, dominated first by the relatively liberal intelligentsia, then by the more authoritarian military, had been established. Domestically, the government strengthened the state by reforms in agriculture, education, and public health. In foreign affairs, it hewed to a pro-Japanese line and thereby Thailand succeeded in escaping Japanese occupation during the war as it had avoided British and French conquests in earlier years. Its smallness made Thailand susceptible to foreign influence — Japanese in the 1930's and early 1940's, British before 1932 and after the war — but it managed to safeguard its sovereignty. In 1946 Thailand became a member of the United Nations, and in 1954 joined the South East Asia Treaty Organization.

Politically Thailand vacillated between democracy and military dictatorship. In 1946 a new constitution provided for a bicameral legislature, with the lower house elective. A military coup d'état in 1947 substituted a new provisional constitution for that of 1946. In 1949 a "permanent" constitution confirmed most of the terms of the provisional constitution, but only two years later, in 1951, another coup d'état reactivated the constitution of 1932. Once again there was a legislature of only one house, chosen partly by election, partly by appointment. Coups continued to bring different personalities to the pinnacle of government, notably Pridi Bhanomyong, leader of the civilian liberals, and Pibul Songgram, leader of the military faction, ousted in 1957 by Lt. General Thanom Kitkhachon, a National-Socialist. The influence of the military remained generally dominant in the postwar period, strengthened by the need to protect Thailand against Communist inroads from abroad. Fortunately there was a steady improvement in economic conditions, partly due to foreign demand for Siamese raw materials and foodstuffs, and partly to American aid; thus, in spite of political tribulations, Thailand attained considerable stability.

In Burma, native interest in politics was relatively slow

to develop. The educated Burmese preferred the road of civil service, even the senior services being open to the natives after 1923. The constitution of that year made the legislature, founded in 1897, elective, even though only half of the ministerial portfolios went to Burmese. Joined with India in 1886 for administrative purposes, Burma became a separate Crown Colony in 1937 with local autonomy, but excessive political faction produced such disunity as to prompt repeated intervention by the British governor.

The Japanese conquest of Burma in 1942–45 shattered British prestige. At the same time it united diverse native elements in common opposition to the invaders and gave the Burmese leaders experience and effective organization. When the British returned after the war they faced a strong coalition of revolutionary forces, the Anti-Fascist People's Freedom League. British attempts to delay the granting of independence until the economy had been reconstructed met with opposition. Accordingly, as native resistance increased, the British granted full independence to Burma in 1948. Unlike India, Burma chose not to remain in the Commonwealth of Nations.

The new republic, the Union of Burma, was over 261,000 square miles in extent; it had a population of nearly twenty million. Its constitution provided it with a popularly elected legislature of two houses, and a president, elected by the two houses, his tenure of office limited to two five-year terms. Independence did not bring internal peace, however. Extremist political groups of various sorts, including two Communist parties, vied for control, pushing the experienced officials who could have provided the needed political stability into the background. Not until 1952 could elections be held.

The policy of Prime Minister U Nu and of the Anti-Fascist People's Freedom League, which gained a majority at the polls in 1952 and again in 1956, was one of moderate socialism. Many British and Indian enterprises were nationalized, but with due compensation and even with foreign assistance. The quick granting of independence and generous British and American aid minimized anti-Westernism in postwar Burma. On the other

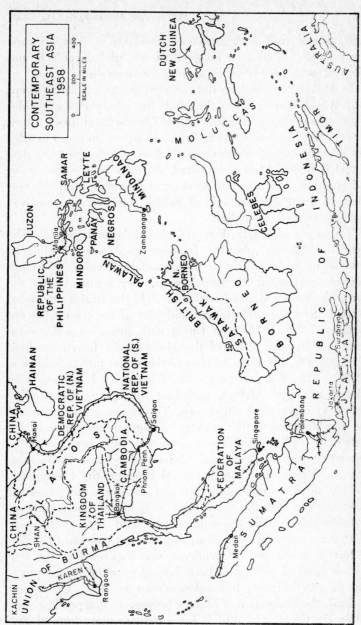

CONTEMPORARY
SOUTHEAST ASIA
1958

SCALE IN MILES
0   200   400

From Alfred Crofts and Percy Buchanan, *A History of the Far East;* copyright, 1958, Longmans, Green & Co., Inc.

hand, preoccupied with economic problems at home, Burma was reluctant to become involved in any global conflicts and followed, whenever possible, a policy of neutralism.

In Malaya, nationalism did not develop to any large extent until World War II. Less than half the inhabitants were Malayan, almost an equal number were Chinese, and about fifteen per cent were Indian, with the British in a position to act as arbiters. The Straits Settlements Crown Colony and nine protectorates, of which British Malaya consisted, were well off economically and enjoyed various public services. In general, until the outbreak of war the advantages of British rule overshadowed the disadvantages of colonialism.

The war completely disrupted the Malayan economy. The economic situation, plus the Japanese awakening of Malayan nationalism, both directly by propaganda and indirectly by oppression, confronted the British when they returned after the war with another colonial crisis. In 1946 the British attempted to weld all of the protectorates and part of the colony (except Singapore) into a Malayan Union with increased self-government; but the opposition of the Malays, who feared for their racial identity, led them to change the union into a federation (1948). This did not please the Chinese and Indians, who wanted a united Malaya, including Singapore, though they wished to retain dual citizenship. The continued allegiance of the non-Malayans to the country of their origin constituted a particularly difficult problem because over forty per cent of the population were Chinese and China had become Communist. The guerrilla warfare which ensued between the Communists and the British complicated (but did not stop) the process of reconstruction. At the same time it hastened the attainment of independence, for the nationalists could argue with some effect that continued colonialism played into Communist hands.

Native desire for independence was expressed in the federal elections of 1955, and the following year the British promised to grant Malaya full independence in 1957. On August 31, 1957, the Federation of Malaya became an independent state within the Commonwealth. It has a parliamentary form of government with the head of the federation elected from among the heads of the various states.

In different parts of Southeast Asia the struggle for independence took different forms. Nonetheless there was a common experience which the peoples of Southeast Asia shared, a common experience which is worth keeping in mind.

1. During the Age of Imperialism the Westerners had reserved for themselves the highest social and economic positions; the former native aristocracy was either "used" or displaced. The end of colonial rule brought an end to the white man's political dominance. Yet Westerners retained control of many large enterprises and thus remained highly influential. During the Age of Imperialism the position of Chinese and Indian businessmen had been strengthened rather than weakened, and they still retained dominant positions in the life of the communities. Like the Westerners, they remained apart by themselves, and upon independence were reluctant to give full allegiance to the new states at the expense of their loyalties to the countries of their origin. Beneath the Westerners and the Indian and Chinese businessmen were the natives, the masses of Southeast Asia. Mixtures of many ethnic elements themselves, they were separated from the Westerners, the Indians, and the Chinese by an economic, social, cultural, religious, and political gulf which had to be bridged before national unity could truly be attained.

2. During the Age of Imperialism the native agricultural economies had been supplemented by raw material and food production geared to export, and thus dependent on world conditions. Independence did not basically change this dependence on export. Yet most foreign trade was in foreign hands. Agricultural reforms, however effective politically, could not alone raise the generally low standard of living. The absence of a native capitalist class demanded government leadership and participation in industrialization and increased production.

3. The disruption of the native economies in the Age of Imperialism did much to undermine age-old ways and traditions. Resistance to new ideas was weakened. The identification of

imperialism and capitalism in native eyes often gave these new ideas a Socialist and Communist tenor.

4. Anti-imperialism and anti-Westernism served as a rallying force for otherwise hostile ideologies: theocratism, nationalism, and Communism. Anti-Western sentiment did not preclude the adoption of Western ideals. The most ardent nationalists were usually men educated in the West. Whether democratic or totalitarian in outlook, they were greatly indebted to Western thought.

5. Independence was not the cure-all of native ills. It was not the end but only the beginning of national struggle. The inhibition of native administration during the Age of Imperialism left the new countries with a shortage of experienced men. The trend was toward democratic government, but the magnitude of the task ahead always left the temptation for quicker, more dramatic measures at the hands of totalitarian leaders.

All the Southeast Asian nations except the Viet Nams have sought and received membership in the United Nations: the Philippines, 1945; Thailand, 1946; Burma, 1948; Indonesia, 1950; Cambodia and Laos, 1955; and the Federation of Malaya, 1957.

CHINA

The victory of Japan over Russia was most notable for its racial implications. But it appeared to be also a victory of westernization over tradition, a victory of constitutional government over absolute monarchy, and the Chinese who looked for a "key" to Japanese success believed they discerned it in Japan's constitution. Thus the adoption of a constitution which would change the outward form of Manchu autocracy became a major concern of Chinese statesmen. In 1906, following a study of other political systems, the Manchu government promised to grant a constitution, and the next year pledged to do so in 1917. Considering the fact that at this time less than one per cent of the populace could read or write, the delay was not unreasonable. As it happened, however, the Chinese revolution of 1911–12 swept the Manchus off the dragon throne.

In the years after the Russo-Japanese War, reforms were instituted in many areas. The content of the civil service examinations was modernized, and military training was improved. The chief obstacle to effective changes was the shortage of

funds, as vested interests resisted the necessary financial reforms. Modernization was slowed also by a lack of follow-
through, stemming from the traditional attitude that a reform
had been effected once it had been proclaimed. Nevertheless,
in 1909 provincial assemblies were convoked and the following
year even a national assembly, and though the powers of these
bodies were limited, it seems likely that the Manchu autocracy would have evolved into a constitutional monarchy had it
not been overthrown.

The Chinese Revolution broke out on October 10 ("Double
Ten"), 1911. Like all great revolutions, it was not the work of
individuals who had conspired to strike on a certain day at a
given hour, but had built up impersonally over a prolonged
period of time, until a number of unforeseen events released
the pent-up tension in a great explosion, the revolutionary
leaders being blown into the forefront of action by events greater
than themselves.

The basic causes of the revolution were much the same as
those that had precipitated the downfall of previous dynasties:
natural calamities such as floods, and the consequent social and
economic dislocation, with famine and banditry ravaging the
country, were traditionally read as signs that a dynasty had
lost the Mandate of Heaven. In addition, there was the increasing burden of taxation, necessitated by the heavy indem-
nities of the Sino-Japanese War and the Boxer Rebellion and
by the cost of various reforms. As nationalist feeling grew, there
was a mounting racial animosity toward all foreigners, including the Manchus. The political agitation of reformers and revolutionaries — constitutional monarchists like K'ang Yu-wei and
Liang Ch'i-ch'ao and republicans like Sun Yat-sen — helped to
undermine public confidence in the established order. In this
work they were aided by the grumbling of young intellectuals,
who enjoyed great respect and influence among the illiterate
masses. Like Japan, the Manchu empire had sent many students abroad to study modern methods. Unlike Japan, however,
the Manchu empire had not given these students, on their return, the jobs and opportunities to put into effect what they

had learned. The resultant loss of support of the majority of young intellectuals was as detrimental to the Manchu government as it was to be to the Nationalist regime in the years after World War II.

The immediate cause of the revolution was the government's railroad policy. Hard pressed financially, it had tried to develop its railway program with local means. The inability of the provinces to raise sufficient capital forced the government to assume the burden itself with foreign aid. But construction of some of the roads had begun already, and the provincial investors, opposed to nationalization of the railways, inflamed public opinion. This was true especially in Chengtu, the capital of Szechwan province. Here famine reigned as the result of the flooding of the Yangtze river, and there were many desperate souls who welcomed any disturbance which might offer them the opportunity to plunder the food shops. When, following a clash between the police and a mob, military reinforcements were rushed to Chengtu from Wuchang, revolutionaries in Wuchang planned an uprising in the weakened city. Before their preparations were complete, a bomb exploded accidentally in one of their hide-outs. The discovery by police of accomplices and of evidence of the plot forced the hand of the revolutionaries. They attacked the office of the viceroy in Wuchang, but were thrown back. That same day several soldiers were executed for attempting to steal a cannon. Aroused, their comrades joined forces with the rebels, and together they captured the office of the viceroy. By the following day, October 11, 1911, the whole city was in their hands.

The fall of Wuchang, the joint capital of the provinces of Hupeh and Hunan, triggered uprisings in other parts of the country, especially in the south, which had been traditionally more anti-Manchu as well as more exposed to the influence of foreign ideas. The viceroy and the commander of the imperial forces in Wuchang had eluded the revolutionaries, but Colonel Li Yüan-hung, second in command, was apprehended and, not untypically, persuaded to lead the revolutionary forces.

The Emperor Kuang Hsü and the Empress Dowager had both

died in 1908. When the revolution broke out, China was ruled by Emperor Hsüan T'ung, aged five, and his regent and advisers. Too weak to cope with the situation themselves, the latter recalled Yüan Shih-k'ai, an official who had been dismissed some years back, and though he took command of the imperial cause and became Prime Minister, he acted without great dispatch or determination.

At the outbreak of the revolution Dr. Sun Yat-sen, the Western-educated "father" of the Chinese Revolution, was not even in China, but he hastened home and took leadership of the republican forces. As Yüan Shih-k'ai and Sun Yat-sen faced each other, they were about evenly matched, for the ardor of the southern rebels was balanced by the experience and authority of the loyalist soldiery in the north. Instead of plunging China into bitter and protracted civil war, the two sides made an ingenious compromise. A republic was established with Yüan Shih-k'ai, the leader of the imperial forces, as president. The child emperor Hsüan T'ung (better known in later years as Mr. Henry Pu-yi, puppet emperor of Manchukuo), was pensioned off liberally, the tomb of his late father was to be completed at state expense, and the five peoples of China — Chinese, Manchus, Moslems, Mongols, and Tibetans — were extended equality of treatment. With the suddenness of a melodrama, but with little bloodshed, the Manchu dynasty came to an end.

The ease with which the revolutionaries overthrew the monarchy was the more startling when compared with the T'ai P'ing rebellion. It was due to the total disintegration of Manchu power and support as well as to the improved means of communication and the superior training of the rebels. Lacking was the anti-Christian feeling of Boxer days, for many of the revolutionary leaders, like Sun, were mission-educated.

But it was one thing to proclaim a republic, another to make it into the democracy Sun had envisioned. The political struggle which developed between Yüan, who wished to be a strong executive, and Sun's adherents, who wanted to dominate Yüan, finally goaded the radicals into another uprising. Yüan was the stronger now, and Sun and other revolutionaries had to seek temporary refuge in Japan. Yüan overreached himself, however, when he tried to become emperor. Rebellions flared up throughout the land and threatened to unseat him. His death in the summer of 1916 inaugurated a decade of chaotic division. Military strong men or "war lords" with their private armies dominated different regions. War lords by themselves and in combination with other war lords in ever-changing configurations fought each other for control of the country. Sun and his republican followers, banded together in the Kuomintang or Nationalist party, succeeded in continuing a republican government in Canton; but not only was it weaker than the group of militarists in the north, it depended itself on the support of local war lords.

As in centuries past, however, political disunity was not a bar to intellectual advance, and the period 1916–27 witnessed the New Culture Movement, commonly called "The Chinese Renaissance." It was born from the realization that the revolution of 1911–12 had failed because China had not been prepared intellectually for the required changes. Thus Chinese spokesmen of the Renaissance, notably Hu Shih, sought to foster a critical outlook, a "transvaluation of values," to rid China of all that was outmoded and introduce new, dominantly Western concepts and values. The attack on Chinese tradition was not confined to Confucian ideology. The whole style of writing was modified — a very important undertaking, because the popularization of the written language helped to bridge the gap between the intellectuals and the masses. On the other hand, the uncompromising stand taken by the intellectuals of the Renaissance may have contributed to the almost complete rejection of Chinese culture in China in our own day.

The adoption of foreign ideas was not then (any more than now) inconsistent with nationalism. The First World War had stirred national consciousness in China, as everywhere. When Japan, taking advantage of Europe's fratricidal struggle, attempted to press upon China the infamous Twenty-One Demands (1915), the Chinese were thereby prompted (partly on the advice of President Woodrow Wilson) to enter the war in order to be represented at the peace conference. The settlement of 1919, whereby the Western Allies handed over to Japan the former German possessions in China, enraged the Chinese. Thousands of students in Peking and other cities staged demonstrations and agitated the populace. The Chinese delegates never signed the Treaty of Versailles.

Mounting antiforeignism reached its height in the summer of 1925, when several Chinese students, demonstrating in the international settlement of Shanghai in support of a strike in a Japanese mill, were killed in a clash with English-officered police. The passionate hatred which the Chinese openly showed at this time was correctly analyzed by John Van Antwerp MacMurray, the American Minister. His observations are well worth recalling, because they apply to a certain extent to the present situation. Pointing out that Chinese aspirations had become intertwined with emotion and that, like other Asians, the Chinese had become increasingly resentful of the "assumed superiority of the white races," he wrote:

> That tendency has been vastly complicated, however, by more subtle elements of feeling latent in the minds of the Chinese and now brought to the surface by an emotional upheaval. Chinese who were heretofore most friendly and congenial with foreigners are now stirred to intolerance and pour out of their memories long stored-up recollections of abuses and indignities on the part of foreigners toward their people — instances of jostling off the sidewalks, of the kicking of rickshaw coolies, and the like. Even though it expresses itself in political terms, the present crisis of feeling, it seems to me, is to be construed as a revulsion against what the individual Chinese feels to be the offense to his personal dignity and self-esteem, implicit in the overbearing attitude of the white man towards the Chinese. It is an inferiority complex which under the stress of an almost nation-wide excitement prompts him to a hysterical self-assertion that is subjective rather than objective and that involves antiforeign feeling only indirectly and as an assertion of self.
>
> This feeling has been further complicated by the fact that thinking Chinese are aware of the failure they are making in the organization of their national life and morbidly conscious of the poor showing that they have made in the eyes of foreign nations.

It is especially true of Chinese human nature that it flinches from recognition of its own deficiencies and by an instinctive subconscious process seeks excuses in the action of others. It is natural and easy for the Chinese to gloss over the miserable political conditions which they realize and resent, by reference to such catchwords as *unequal treaties* or *foreign imperialism*.[1]

Meanwhile Sun Yat-sen had revitalized his party with foreign help. He had failed to obtain this help from the United States and the other Western democracies, who found it more convenient to deal with the strong, seemingly better established military government in the north. As the German humorist Erich Kästner generalizes in his satirical play, *Die Schule der Diktatoren:* "The foreign countries recognize a government only when it is consolidated. And a government is consolidated only when it is recognized by the foreign countries." In desperation Sun had turned to the only country which had offered him the needed aid, indeed had been eager to help: the Soviet Union.

The Communist revolution in Russia had followed the Chinese revolution by six years, but it had been more successful in gaining control of the whole country, and by now Russia could offer Sun the services of professional revolutionists, skilled in proven Communist tactics. Ostracized by the West, Russia herself welcomed an ally. Moreover, it was a tenet of Communist doctrine that the prosperity of the capitalistic West rested on the exploitation of China and other colonial or semicolonial countries. To strengthen the position of these nations vis-à-vis the West, be it even through the support of an anti-Communist regime, was regarded as tantamount to pulling the rug out from under Western capitalism. Russia's position was strengthened by the fact that she had been excluded from the Paris Peace Conference, at which the Allies had so aroused Chinese antagonism. Moreover, since the Chinese had taken advantage of the Russian revolution to strip Russia of her special privileges and concessions in China, Russia could the more read-

---

[1] United States, State Department, *Papers Relating to the Foreign Relations of the United States, With the Annual Message of the President* (Washington: U. S. Government Printing Office, 1925), p. 799.

ily renounce in theory what she had already lost in fact. "If the people of China wish to become free, like the Russian people, and be spared the lot prepared for them by the Allies at Versailles, which would make of China a second Korea or a second India," the Soviet government exhorted, "let it understand that its only ally and brother in its struggle for national freedom are the Russian workers and peasants and their Red Army."

The communization of China was not the goal of Sun nor, for the moment, of the Soviet advisers. To be sure, Sun no longer hoped for immediate democracy, and envisioned three stages through which the Chinese revolution must pass — a period of military action, a period of political tutelage, and, only then, the period of democracy. But his goal remained his Three People's Principles: nationalism, democracy, and people's livelihood — a form of centralized, democratic socialism, but not Communism. What Sun and his brother-in-law Chiang K'ai-shek wanted from Communism were its techniques of political subversion of the military opponent and, upon victory, its framework (not ideology) of political structure. Chiang K'ai-shek himself studied Russian tactics in Moscow for a year before becoming president of the Whampoa Military Academy, the West Point of the Nationalist revolution, with Chou En-lai in charge of the political education of the cadets. That year, in 1924, the Kuomintang itself was reorganized with the assistance of Mikhail Borodin in the image of the Russian Communist party. On his death in 1925, Sun Yat-sen was enshrined like Lenin, and like Lenin passed into legend as the superhuman fountainhead of revolution.

As in Russia, the inevitable struggle for succession following the death of the "father" of the revolution resulted in the victory of the more nationalistic contender, in China's case, Chiang K'ai-shek. It is of interest to note here that part of the struggle between Joseph Stalin and Leon Trotsky in Russia was over the issue of Communist cooperation with the Nationalists in China. Trotsky, the idealistic world revolutionary, objected to such cooperation; Stalin, the realistic "Russia-firster," defended it as a temporary expedient.

In 1926–27, under the guidance of the Soviet General Galen

(Vasilii Blücher), and with the assistance of countless Communist organizers, the Nationalist forces launched upon the military conquest of the northern regions. Thus China was reunified, not by the ballot box but by political subversion and the sword. But before the reunification of China had been completed (1928), Chiang K'ai-shek, fearful lest Soviet guidance mature into Soviet dictation, abruptly turned against the Communists, machine-gunned many of his comrades-in-arms, and expelled the Russian advisers. Friction between the left and right wings of the Kuomintang had been increasing for some time, and it is likely that the Communists would have discarded Chiang like a squeezed-out lemon had he not squeezed and discarded first. Relations between Chiang and the Soviet government, in spite of repeated incidents and a temporary official "break" (1927–32), remained remarkably good under the circumstances. Indeed, the Soviet government until the closing days of World War II generally continued to support Chiang more than the Chinese Communists, for the idealism of world revolution had been overtaken by the realities of national security, and the Soviet Union needed a strong China as a buffer against Japan. Until 1945 Chiang seemed the only man capable of rallying his countrymen in common resistance to Japanese aggression. Nevertheless Chiang K'ai-shek's double cross, however justifiable from the Nationalist point of view, laid the foundations for that bitter personal hatred and mistrust which in later years made any genuine compromise agreement between the Communists and Nationalists impossible.

The Nationalist government which Chiang K'ai-shek established in 1928–29 at Nanking was not in complete control of China. The Communists who survived Chiang's coup organized a Chinese soviet republic in Kiangsi in the south (1931). Hard pressed there by the Nationalist forces, they withdrew in the famous "Long March" of over six thousand miles to Shensi province in the northwest, where they proclaimed another soviet republic (1936). Apart from the Communists, Chiang also met resistance from war lords in various parts of China. In fact, he never really gained complete control over all of China.

The Nationalist republic was not a democracy. It did not claim to be one. It had officially progressed from Sun Yat-sen's first stage of military conquest to his second stage of political tutelage. Various efforts were made to prepare China for constitutional government, but essentially it remained a one-party dictatorship, if not a one-family dictatorship, with relatives of the Methodist "Soong Dynasty" in key positions: Sun Yat-sen, Chiang K'ai-shek, and H. H. Kung were husbands of the Soong sisters, and brothers-in-law of T. V. Soong.

In its early days the Kuomintang had been full of ideas for economic reforms and very definitely had a radical tinge. But following the break with the Communists and the realization that economic reforms could not be carried out without basic social changes which the key supporters of the party were not willing to accept, the Kuomintang became increasingly conservative. Like the National Socialist party of Germany in later years, it became increasingly more Nationalist and less Socialist.

But a democracy is not made overnight. The Chinese not only lacked the necessary background for responsible democratic government, but they associated parliamentary government with the remembered chaos of the period after 1912. All things considered, in spite of obvious shortcomings, the Nationalist regime in the early years of its rule gave China the most efficient and progressive government she had ever enjoyed. If anyone deserves special blame for its failure to mature into something more advanced, it is neither Chiang nor the Communists (nor the American State Department), but the Japanese, who struck in 1931, only three years after the real founding of Nationalist China, and continued to hammer away at China for the next fourteen years.

At first Japan drove into Manchuria and a part of Outer Mongolia, and established the puppet state of Manchukuo, with Mr. Henry Pu-yi, the last Manchu emperor, as nominal sovereign. It soon became obvious that no Chinese government, once it had the necessary power, would tolerate Japanese retention of this region, and it was equally obvious that the Japanese had still further designs. A Chinese boycott of Japanese products, ships, and banks provoked a Japanese naval bombardment of Shanghai and Nanking in 1932. Aside from a general predilection for fishing in troubled waters (especially when the Western powers were preoccupied with economic depression or war), Japan dreamed of becoming the workshop of Asia, and this she could be only as long as China, with her greater resources and manpower, did not industrialize. Japan wanted to secure for herself raw materials and markets, since the protective tariffs in the West were a genuine threat to her economy, but the Co-prosperity Sphere which she exalted in her propaganda would have done more than that. It would have perpetuated Japan's position of industrial dominance.

So great was anti-Japanese feeling in China, as the result of Japanese aggression, that Chiang K'ai-shek's policy of appeasement — whether or not it was logically justified by China's military weakness and the danger of Communist revolution — seriously lowered the prestige of his government. In 1936 he was kidnapped by one of his own generals and forced to come to terms with the Communists in a united front against Japan. If the Japanese had looked with apprehension on the prospect of a united China, they looked with real dread on the possibility of a united China dominated by the Communists. In July, 1937, they struck again, this time in full force.

In the Second Sino-Japanese War which ensued, the Japanese were not so readily successful as in 1894–95. To be sure, they made enormous gains and captured the most desirable parts of China, but Chiang refused to surrender or compromise. The Nationalist government evacuated the coastal provinces and cities; it moved ever more into the interior, trading space for time, and with it moved millions of Chinese soldiers, workers, and students.

The impact of this great migration cannot be exaggerated. Here was a basic transformation of Chinese society, a break with local and family ties, a break with the whole past. Into the backward hinterlands the students brought radical Western ideas, and the workers with government help set up cooperative workshops to supply Free China with the necessary arms and commodities. At the same time, however, the Nationalist government was separated from its erstwhile financial supporters in the coastal cities. Highly conservative by American standards, these big businessmen with their Western education had yet constituted a pillar of support relatively liberal when compared with the big land lords of the interior provinces on whom the Nationalist government was now forced to lean. The repeated changes in capitals and government offices and positions, to say nothing of the constantly shifting population, made elections impossible. The same men remained in office for years without the vital guidance and control of the electorate. Corruption was a natural outcome. Thus while the ravages and changes brought by the war called for drastic measures and undermined the native conservatism of the peasantry, the government was growing increasingly reactionary, inefficient, and corrupt. Its ultimate fall was one of the costs of the war.

Meanwhile the Communists were strengthening their position. The guerrilla tactics which they perfected in their struggle with the Japanese were to be no less effective later in their struggle with the Nationalists. The war gave them the opportunity to disseminate their ideology and to organize support. But above all, as pointed out already, the war was a revolution in itself. All the Communists had to do, as the Nationalists lost contact with the masses, was to ride into power on the crest of the revolutionary wave. When civil war flared up again after the defeat of Japan by the Allied powers in 1945, the Chinese Communists emerged victorious, not because the peasants had become converted to dialectical materialism, nor because of the initial strength of the Communist armies, nor because of Russian aid, but because the Nationalist regime, like the Manchu dynasty in 1911, had lost the confidence of the people. The Nationalist administration which moved into Shanghai after the Japanese surrender, for example, compared unfavorably even with the hated Japanese occupation. The Communists, on the other hand, put their best foot forward. In Changsha, Chinese houses requisitioned by the Japanese and subsequently confiscated by the Nationalists as enemy property were returned by the Com-

COMMUNIST CHINA IN 1951

From Meribeth E. Cameron, Thomas H. D. Mahoney and George E. McReynolds, *China, Japan and the Powers;* copyright 1952 The Ronald Press Company.

munists to the original owners. Their soldiery was well disciplined, paid for what it took, and did not abuse the populace. Some of the bigger land lords were killed, but on the whole the Communist approach at the time showed the velvet glove rather than the mailed fist. That the Communists had other plans in store for the future, most people did not know.

It was time for a change, any change. There was no effective third force of middle-of-the-roaders to furnish guidance. Increasingly the students and the white-collar workers, alienated by the stifling activity of the Nationalist secret police and hard pressed by runaway inflation, drifted to the left. The staggering difficulties of postwar readjustment and the spreading unrest were signs that the Nationalist government had lost the Mandate of Heaven. American efforts to bolster the Nationalist regime were of no avail. In a way they did more harm than good to the Nationalist cause, lessening the government's sense of urgency to make drastic reforms, and identifying it in Chinese eyes, however unjustly, with foreign domination. It was one of the great ironies of the civil war that the Communists emerged in the public mind as the nationalists of China. The Chinese had never been prone to fight for lost causes. As the storm of Communist revolution increased in velocity, the discredited Nationalist government collapsed like a house of cards. In October, 1949, the Communist leader, Mao Tse-tung, proclaimed the new People's Republic of China.

There has been much bitter controversy in the United States as to the true nature of the Communist regime in China. American observers have been accused of treachery and willful deceit. Actually the discrepancy in accounts is less partisan than chronological. What was true of the Communists in China in the 1930's was no longer true in the 1940's. Without changing his own mind, without being inconsistent, the same observer could thus come up with different pictures of Chinese Communism at different times. The date of publication of any description of Communist China is therefore of particular importance. For example, the writings of Lord Lindsay of Birker, a British Socialist authority on China and a member of the House of Lords, run the gamut from sympathy to revulsion. The more firmly entrenched the Communists became in China, the more drastic and uncompromising their measures. Mao Tse-tung was master of the country, and though in 1959 he resigned his position of Chairman of the Chinese People's Republic and was succeeded by Liu Shao-ch'i, an eminent Marxist theoretician who had studied in Moscow, he continued to dominate all events as the Great Leader.

By the end of the 1950's the Chinese revolution had become

the most profound cultural upheaval of all times. In its effort to harness the entire Chinese population to a great industrial "leap forward," designed to put China once again in the forefront of civilization and power, the Communist government has deemed it necessary (like Shih Huang Ti, the founder of the first Chinese empire) to cut all ideological ties with the past. Not only is history literally being rewritten, but the family, the traditional nucleus of Chinese loyalty and devotion, is being broken up and superseded by communes and other economic and political forms of organization. The pace and degree of the changes are far more extreme than ever attempted in the U.S.S.R. To some extent this is so because, in spite of the rejection of the past, many aspects of Communism — government planning, an elite of officials who indoctrinate the public, forced labor, and emphasis on duty above personal interests — find a common chord in Chinese tradition. But a more important factor is the resurgence in almost psychopathic form of the feeling of national reassertion, described by the American minister in 1925. For a century the Chinese had been pushed around and humiliated by foreigners. Now there was a chance to pay them back with dividends.

If this feeling is kept in mind, many Chinese actions become understandable. Americans are frustrated by the fact that "reasonable" proposals are turned down by Communist negotiators. But often the Chinese say "no" not because the American proposal is unacceptable, but because it is the American proposal. They say "no" because we say "yes," "yes" because we say "no." Childish? Immature? Perhaps. But there is a deep satisfaction in being able to pay back long-suffered indignities, especially of a national or racial character.

Within China the consolidation of military power was welcomed as an insurance against continued unrest. It must be remembered that China had been in a state of turmoil for practically half a century, if not longer, and that stability was more in demand at the moment than freedom. At the same time the Chinese were conscious of the fact that in the West military prowess had long been a yardstick of respect. They were convinced that the arrogance of military swagger would be more effective in regaining for China her rightful place in world affairs than had been the polite sophistication of the more humane but powerless Confucianism.

The Nationalist government had been driven off the continent to the island of Formosa (Taiwan), regained from Japan in 1945. Its chances of winning back control of the mainland appeared nil, even if Communism were to encounter increased opposition; its chances of remaining outside the Communist orbit indefinitely were not bright. Its continued existence as a political bastion may or may not be crucial, for Free China, as Taiwan calls itself, is still not very free politically; but Communist determination to obliterate the past has invested Taiwan with a new and vital role, that of preserving and propagating Chinese culture for the benefit of mankind.

AFRICA

The character of European rule in Africa differed from region to region. In some colonies it was enlightened, in others less so. But whether Western rule was direct or indirect, enlightened or not, it necessarily led to the introduction of Western ideas. One of these was nationalism. Africa had never been united, and the "partition" of the continent had not materially increased disunion. To be sure, nationalism as fostered by the colonial powers had as its purpose loyalty to the "mother country." The natives of French Africa, for example, were taught about "our ancestors, the Gauls." But the humiliation of the white man in the Russo-Japanese War and the rise of "colored" peoples throughout the world in the twentieth century stirred African hopes for independence, with Western means of communication, both physical and intellectual, becoming arteries of a new nationalism. Western dominance had been made possible by African weakness; it had been facilitated by the superiority of European administration to tribal rule. But with the education of native leaders abroad — in England, France, and the United States — a new standard of comparison was provided, and colonial government, in the light of Western democracy, became increasingly objectionable.

The tide of world events, moreover, was running against colonialism in Africa. The employment of native troops against white opponents in World War I contaminated the superior status of all Westerners. The victory of the Allied powers stripped Germany of her colonies. German Southwest Africa was transferred to the Union of South Africa; Togoland and Kamerun were both divided, as mandates, between Great Britain and France; the bulk of German East Africa passed to Great Britain (the Tanganyika Territory), with the regions in the northwest (Ruanda-Urundi) becoming a Belgian mandate. Whatever bonds of loyalty had developed were thus loosened. The acceptance of the principle of national self-determination in Europe hastened the breakdown of colonialism everywhere. In 1919 the first of a series of pan-African conferences, advocating self-determination for the natives, was held in Paris. Meanwhile Europeans themselves became increasingly concerned with native rights and with Western responsibility both to learn more about native society and to improve local conditions. But it was really not until after World War II that Africa, trailing behind Asia, sought freedom from the embrace of a dying colonialism.

If World War II heightened African demands for independence, it also underlined the continent's importance to Europe. The Japanese occupation of Allied possessions in Southeast Asia and the Far East inflated Africa's value as source of tropical raw materials. Meanwhile Axis entrenchment in North Africa seriously threatened British and French communications with the Orient, near and far. African troops, trained in mounting numbers, contributed to Allied victories not only on the African continent but in Burma as well.

World War II was a struggle for freedom. In its origin it was a struggle against Nazi racism and tyranny, but once the banner of freedom has been unfurled, its appeal is universal. The ideological opposition of the Common Man to the Super Man was given universal application: defeat of the Super Man would secure the status of the Common Man everywhere. Self-government became the goal not only of native patriots, but of an increasing number of colonial administrators, and promises of social, economic, and political reforms in Africa after the war were generally made. Altogether, the humiliating appeasement of Fascist aggressors throughout most of the 1930's, the renewed humiliation of the white man at the hands of the Japanese, and the recurrence of fratricidal struggle within Europe contributed to the wane of Western influence. African participation in the war boosted African military experience and self-confidence.

The Charter of the United Nations, formulated in 1945, transformed the African mandates of the Allies into "trust territories." The authority of the administrating power was more narrowly circumscribed by international supervision in the form of a Trusteeship Council, and the colonial powers generally committed themselves to work toward the self-government of their colonies. Africans had been prepared unevenly for independence. In some places the granting of immediate self-government would have been an irresponsible act, bound to enslave the populace in local despotism and chaos. In other regions only selfishness dictated the continuation of colonial rule.

Great Britain, at the end of World War II, possessed Gambia, Sierra Leone, the Gold Coast, and Nigeria in West Africa; Kenya, Uganda, Tanganyika, British Somaliland, and the Anglo-Egyptian Sudan in East Africa; Northern Rhodesia, Southern Rhodesia, Nyasaland, Bechuanaland, Basutoland and Swaziland in Central and South Africa. Togoland and the Cameroons were under her supervision; the Union of South Africa was a self-governing dominion within the British Commonwealth. Of the colonies the Gold Coast, with its prosperous cocoa production and small-scale native agriculture, was perhaps the most advanced economically and politically. Vigorous and at times violent agitation brought it increasing constitutional rights until, in 1954, the legislature and the cabinet were all African, though defense and foreign affairs remained in British hands. Under

the leadership of Prime Minister Kwame Nkrumah the Gold
Coast continued on the road to modernization and self-government. In spring of 1957, it became the first independent
sovereign African state within the British Commonwealth, re-
named Ghana, in memory of the old African stat   and including
the former trusteeship of Togoland. Two days after its independence Ghana became a member of the United Nations.
Ghana had "graduated" to freedom:

MARCH 6, 1957

Let Ghana prove a point: that to be free
A nation must have served a tutelage,
Be ruled to know what government can be,
Be taught by elders how to come of age.

Nkrumah knew injustice in the raw
And learned oppression in a prison cell,
But now he wears the wig of British law
And Britain's Parliament is his as well.

And he can prove that banners, blood, and hate
Are not the womb of stable liberty
But only kickings of an embryo state
Far from fruition and maturity.

Nkrumah knows; he learned the hardest way
To set his people free: not overnight
In a blind rage, but on that hard-won day
When they had graduated to the right.[1]

Nigeria, the largest colonial territory of Great Britain, made
considerable progress in the twentieth century, but its political
aspirations were hampered by the diversity of its population,
cultures, and interests. The monarchistic Moslem Fulani and
Hausa in the north wished to preserve their own culture; the
business-minded Ibos in the south were eager students of Western civilization. They and the Yoruba in the south were pri-

[1] Signed SEC. *The Reporter*, March 21, 1957. Reprinted by permission.

marily pagan or Christian in faith, set apart from the Fulani and Hausa by religion as well as interest in Western civilization. The incorporation of the diverse peoples of this region in the Colony and Protectorate of Nigeria in 1914 was the first step toward self-government; a new constitution in 1922 was the second. After World War II, in 1946, yet another constitution was granted, leading toward self-government, with safeguards for minorities, by way of federalism. In 1952 increased autonomy was given the Nigerian federation, with taxpayers participating in government. The constitution of 1954 broadened the federation's self-government, and in 1957 its first prime minister was appointed, but it remained hampered by internal divisions and trailed behind Ghana in obtaining full sovereignty.

In British East Africa, where divergent altitudes and temperatures encouraged the settlement of a variety of peoples, white colonization made important advances in the early twentieth century, particularly in Kenya (once known as the East African Protectorate). The white settlers, whose heavy investment of money and labor was responsible for the agricultural development of the highlands, sought to arrogate all government to themselves. They opposed no less the native-protecting policies of the British government than the aspirations of the Africans and the immigrant Indians. In the wake of World War II, real and imaginary native grievances were galvanized into violent anti-Westernism by the Mau Mau, a secret terrorist society; thousands of white settlers and natives who refused to join in ousting the foreigners were murdered before Mau Mau power was crushed by the British army. In 1937 a certain amount of local government had been extended to local native councils. The granting of a new constitution in 1952 and of liberalizing amendments in 1954 broadened native participation in the colony's government, whose Council of Ministers was to include Europeans, Asians, and Africans.

The transition to native rule, however unevenly made, was almost universal throughout Africa. The king of Buganda, whose land constituted the core of the Uganda protectorate, was confirmed not only in the title of "Highness" and a salute of nine

guns, but in the assistance of native ministers; and the Legis-
lative Council, which in 1921 had been composed of six
Europeans, consisted in 1955 of sixty members, half of them
African, the remainder European and Asian.

In Tanganyika, administered by Britain as a United Nations
trust territory, the Legislative Council was divided equally between Europeans, Africans, and Asians. Knowledge of the
English language was not a requirement for membership.

In Central Africa, Southern Rhodesia, Northern Rhodesia,
and Nyasaland were joined in a federation. The constitution of
1953 granted virtual self-government to the Federation of Rhodesia and Nyasaland, with local affairs in the hands of the
respective territories. Self-government was neither complete nor
equal, since Nyasaland remained a protectorate, but there were
prospects for a revision of the constitution in the near future.

A different pattern was unfolding in the Union of South
Africa. Though a part of the British Commonwealth and fully
self-governing, its white settlers were predominantly descendants
of the Dutch Boers and were as determined as ever to exclude
the natives from government and church. At a time when racial
barriers were being lowered elsewhere, the white "Afrikaners"
of the Union, under the leadership of Dr. Daniel Malan and his
successors, tightened their control over the black Africans. To
the Afrikaners nationalism meant *apartheid* (segregation) and
white supremacy; to the African multitudes it meant something
quite different, if indeed not the opposite. Afrikaner policy
aroused concern among other European inhabitants, who realized that the pressure mounting beneath the lid of white
supremacy was nearing the explosion point.

France, at the end of World War II, owned French Morocco,
Algeria, Tunisia, French West Africa, French Somaliland,
and Madagascar, and exercised a mandate over the Cameroons
and Togoland. The ultimate objective of French policy was the
assimilation and integration of these lands with France, rather
than self-government and a loosening of ties. Concentrating on
their possessions in the north, the French made many economic
advances. Politically they dominated the scene. Native voices

were raised for greater participation in government, but the French envisaged any reforms only within the framework of the French imperial bloc. The Constitution of the Fourth Republic (1946) created a French Union, of which the overseas territories were an integral part, with representation in both the French parliament and the Assembly of the Union. Again, as so often in European colonial history, it was a case of too little offered too late to satisfy the leaping appetite for independence.

Dissatisfaction with French policy came to a head in Algeria. Though racial discrimination was at a minimum (culture rather than color being the mark of distinction), Algerian Arab nationalists and French militarists locked forces in a deadly combat that killed thousands of people, tied down a large part of the French army, and threatened to engulf North Africa and France in chaos. France's Fourth Republic came tumbling down, and in 1958 General Charles de Gaulle became president of the Fifth Republic, promising to extend to the people of Algeria "full citizenship" and implying Algerian self-determination. Once aroused, however, nationalism is not easily assuaged, and extremists on both sides continued to delay a solution of the Algerian problem. Given the opportunity to vote on the new French constitution — with the clear understanding that secession from France would entail economic isolation and the end of French aid — most of the African territories chose to continue their association with France. Only Guinea rejected the constitution and on October 2, 1958, became an independent republic. Gabon, Chad, and Middle Congo (Equatorial Africa), Mauretania (West Africa), and Ubangi-Shari (Equatorial Africa) voted in November and December of the same year to become republics within the French community: the Middle Congo became the Republic of Congo; Mauretania, the Islamic Republic of Mauretania; and Ubangi-Shari, the Central African Republic. The French Cameroons were granted internal autonomy and promised independence, if so voted in a referendum in 1960. The vote was for independence, and Cameroon took its place in the roster of nations. The Togoland trusteeship was to end in the same year.

AFRICA IN 1958

From *The United States and Africa;* copyright, 1958, The American
Assembly, Columbia University.

The trend was universal. In Libya, in 1951, the British
Residents in Tripolitania and Cyrenaica and the French Resi-
dent in the Fezzan gave up their authority in compliance with a
directive of the United Nations, and Libya became an independent, sovereign federal kingdom. Tunisia gained full internal
autonomy in 1955; independence from France in 1956; and in
1957 abolished her monarchy and became a sovereign independent republic. In 1956 France and Spain terminated their

protectorates over Morocco, and the international status of Tangier was brought to an end, Morocco becoming a sovereign independent monarchy. The same year the British relinquished their hold on the Sudan, and Sudan became an independent republic. Egypt had been an outright British protectorate from 1914 to 1922. Thereafter the British hold had loosened, though the strategic importance of the Suez Canal had brought back British troops, notably in World War II and during the Suez crisis of 1956. British forces finally withdrew in 1956, and in 1958 Egypt joined with Syria in the United Arab Republic. In 1959 the Belgian government committed itself to organize in the Belgian Congo "a democracy capable of exercising sovereignty and making decisions about its independence." On January 27, 1960, Belgian and Congolese leaders agreed that the Belgian Congo would become independent on June 30.

At the outbreak of World War II only three African states had been independent — the Union of South Africa, Liberia, and Ethiopia (Abyssinia) — and the latter had been overrun by Mussolini's forces in 1935. By 1960 more than half of Africa consisted of independent states. Only four African states were charter members of the United Nations in 1945: Egypt, Ethiopia, Liberia, and the Union of South Africa. As other states achieved independence, they too were admitted to membership: Libya, 1955; Morocco, Sudan, and Tunisia, 1956; Ghana, 1957; Guinea, 1958.

Egypt's attempts to whip up Arab nationalism and bring about a pan-Arab federation under Egyptian leadership made little headway in the late 1950's, but a new identification of former colonial and semi-colonial peoples with each other did stir Asia and Africa into a cooperation of momentous possibilities. In the summer of 1955, representatives of the leading nations of Asia and Africa met at Bandung, Indonesia, in the first of a series of Afro-Asian meetings, designed to make common cause in advancing the welfare of the non-Western peoples. In December, 1958, Asian and African chambers of commerce met in conference "to meet the challenge of the European Market and other foreign economic blocs"; and in February,

1959, the Afro-Asian Peoples' Solidarity Council, representing some forty African and Asian nations, met in Egypt and resolved to form a special section of its secretariat to "actively help the freedom movements in the still dependent countries in Africa."

The days of white domination in Africa were numbered. Would the pendulum swing the other way? Arnold Toynbee, the celebrated English historian, has aptly summarized the dilemma confronting the European settlers.

> Either they must resign themselves to the prospect that, sooner or later, they will have to accept the status of an unprivileged minority among a majority whom they now feel to be inferior to them culturally, or they must try to hold on to their present supremacy by main force against a rising tide of revolt against their domination. The second course would obviously be fatal for the minority, for, even if its belief in its own present cultural superiority is justified, numbers will tell in the long run, considering that culture is contagious and that an ascendancy based on cultural superiority is therefore a wasting asset. On the other hand, voluntary abdication in favour of a majority whom one feels to be one's inferiors is a very hard alternative for human pride to accept.[2]

By the middle of the twentieth century it was clear that the impact of the West on Africa had been shattering. Ancient beliefs had been smashed but no moral system had taken their place. The religion of the colonial powers had helped to destroy the old gods, but it had not prevented the exploitation of the natives (indeed, in the hands of Afrikaners, had advanced biblical "documentation" of the black man's inferiority) and was not a popular substitute. Science, Standard of Living, and Nationalism had become new, amoral gods.

Nationalism had been embraced more as a means to independence and freedom from white domination than as an end in itself. Throughout much of Africa, the concept of the nation-state was not deeply rooted: the old medieval native kingdoms

[2] Arnold J. Toynbee, "History's Warning to Africa," *Optima*, IX, No. 2 (June, 1959), 55–56.

had disappeared even from memory, and the boundaries imposed by nineteenth-century imperialism had been dictated only by the reach and grasp of the Europeans. Further development toward some larger pan-African amalgam or federation was not beyond possibility. Ghana and Guinea in 1958 announced a provisional agreement looking toward a union of West African states; and on January 7, 1960, Prime Minister Nkrumah publicly expressed Ghana's willingness to submerge herself in an African union to avoid the "Balkanization" of Africa. Ghana's new republican constitution would make provision for the surrender of the state's sovereignty to a union of West and East African states.

Democracy leaves it to the people to draw up their own blueprints for their political and social governance. The work requires experience, skill, and education; it is slow, laborious, and devoid of glamour. Limited in experience, the Africans have been tempted to seek ready-made blueprints for a modern society. There has been the temptation to copy somebody else's plan, good or bad, simply because it is a plan, on the assumption that any plan is better than none. In Africa, as in other underdeveloped parts of the world beyond Europe, there is a potential ready audience for the hucksters of Communism, with their social, economic, and political blueprints, prepared abroad, like the treaties of the old imperialism.

The peoples of Africa are at last moving into the focus of world history. Africa's past is only now being rediscovered; the shape of Africa's future is only now beginning to take form.

EPILOGUE: PART THREE

Japan's victory over Russia in 1905 heralded the resurgence of Asia. Japanese victories in the early 1940's sounded the trumpet call for national reassertion throughout the world beyond Europe. Japan's own defeat and unconditional surrender did not reverse the process. The seeds of her idea, "Asia for

Asians," had taken root and grown to gigantic proportions. Japan's defeat was Asia's victory.

"Asia" is a geographical concept. Historically, culturally, racially, it does not represent a whole. The contrasting of "East" and "West" leaves the impression that the "East," like the "West," has a common heritage of values and experiences. This is misleading. The only real unity of the Orient inheres in the fact that it is not the Occident. The great diversity of the non-Western world — not only the differences between the Near East and the Far East, or between Asia and Africa, but within the same regions or countries themselves — cannot be overemphasized. Genuinely noble American plans of economic aid to the underdeveloped countries have fallen short of fulfillment because the differences of conditions, needs, and aspirations within the various regions have not been sufficiently appreciated.

In the 1940's and 1950's the peoples of the world beyond Europe found a common denominator in anticolonialism and, because colonialism had been predominantly Western, in anti-Westernism. Many Westerners would have slept less soundly had they been aware of the intensity with which the majority of mankind hated their white skin. The fact that discrimination was not peculiar to the West did not blot out the memory of personal and national humiliation suffered at the hands of white sahibs. By extension, a Brahman, who in his own country eschewed contact with men of lower caste, might take personal offense at American discrimination against Negroes. Though in the United States he himself might be treated as "white," he often identified himself, however light his own skin, with the "colored" peoples of the world. This emotional identification of non-Western peoples with each other was one of the most significant trends of the 1940's and 1950's. The efforts of the Russians to identify their country with Asia were only partly successful. They too were predominantly white. This situation played into Chinese hands, and Communist China threatened to become not only a major industrial power but the ideological fountainhead of Asian and African revolution. Chinese pronouncements on Hungarian, Polish, and German happenings underlined the fact that Asian aspirations were not confined to the expulsion of the foreigners. Henceforth the non-Western peoples would take an active part in world affairs.

But the attainment of independence sapped anticolonialism of its political utility. The mounting nationalism which had united the colonial peoples in their antipathy to the imperialist powers began to pit them against each other as the new nations pursued their respective interests. Chinese subjugation of Tibet and Chinese violation of the Burmese and Indian frontiers shocked Indian leaders into the belated realization that the greatest threat to Indian security lay no longer in the West. Irritated by Chinese attempts to camouflage their own ambitions with ceaseless tirades against British imperialism, Prime Minister Nehru, himself an old opponent of British imperialism, publicly asked: "Was the present big and colossal Chinese State born out of the head of Brahma? How did it grow big and great? Surely in the past it was due to the ability of its people and the conquests of its warriors, in other words to Chinese imperialism."

In 1945 the United States, unlike most other Western powers, enjoyed the esteem of Asian leaders, for its Declaration of Independence furnished them with inspiration and slogans for their own struggle. It was the tragedy of the postwar world that the Americans, the original and true revolutionaries, became afraid (temporarily but fatally) of their own ideals and thereby forfeited revolutionary leadership in most regions to Communists and ultra-nationalists, who led their countries to independence but not to freedom, as the United States might have done. American programs of economic aid, however useful, were often more in the nature of relief than of long-term development. But if the United States in the late 1940's and 1950's lost ground in the struggle with world Communism by not doing enough, it appeared at the onset of the 1960's that the Communist powers had begun to hurt themselves by doing too much. Rapid economic advance remained the goal of the peoples of the world beyond Europe, but they were beginning to examine more closely the price exacted by Communism.

BIBLIOGRAPHICAL NOTE

The World Beyond Europe is merely an introduction to a vast subject. The sources listed below elaborate on the topics covered. Throughout, the general reader has been kept in mind.

GENERAL

Two geographies are convenient introductions to Asia: *Asia East by South. A Cultural Geography* by J. E. Spencer (New York: Wiley, 1954) and *The Pattern of Asia*, edited by Norton Ginsburg (Englewood Cliffs: Prentice-Hall, 1958). The most recent general account of East Asia up to the early nineteenth century is Edwin O. Reischauer and John K. Fairbank, *History of East Asian Civilization*, vol. I: *Traditional East Asia* (Boston: Houghton Mifflin, 1960). An older satisfactory account is G. Nye Steiger, *A History of the Far East* (Boston: Ginn, 1944). A less detailed survey of the same region, with greater emphasis on the modern period, is Kenneth Scott Latourette, *A Short History of the Far East* (3rd ed., New York: Macmillan, 1957). The most detailed and up-to-date one-volume survey of Far Eastern international relations since the nineteenth century is *A History of the Far East in Modern Times* by Harold M. Vinacke (6th ed., New York: Appleton-Century-Crofts, 1959). A simpler coverage of the same period is provided in *The Far East; A History of the Impact of the West on Eastern Asia* by Paul H. Clyde (3rd ed., Englewood Cliffs: Prentice-Hall, 1958) and in *China, Japan and the Powers* by Meribeth E. Cameron, Thomas H. D. Mahoney, and George E. McReynolds (New York: Ronald Press, 1952). An introduction to the world beyond Europe since World War II is given in *The Nature of the Non-Western World* by Vera Micheles Dean and others (New York: New American Library [a Mentor pocketbook], 1957). A detailed examination of East Asia since World War II is *Far Eastern Politics in the Postwar Period* by Harold M. Vinacke (New York: Appleton-Century-Crofts, 1956). Political structures are explained in *Major Governments of Asia*, edited by George McTurnan Kahin (Ithaca: Cornell University Press, 1958). The ever changing frontiers of the world beyond Europe may be followed clearly in the *Atlas of World History*, edited by R. R. Palmer and others (New York: Rand McNally, 1957).

The problem of understanding different cultures is put forth briefly by Georges Fradier in *East and West — Towards Mutual Understanding?* (Paris, 1959; a free UNESCO pamphlet). Brief, readable analyses of American dealings with Asia since World War II are to be found in *Wanted: An Asian Policy* by Edwin O. Reischauer (New York: Knopf, 1955); *The American Record in the Far East, 1945–1951* by Kenneth Scott Latourette (New York: Macmillan, 1952); *The United States and the Far East 1945–1951* by Harold M. Vinacke (Stanford: Stanford University Press, 1952); *U.S. Policy in Asia*, edited by William W. Wade (New York: H. W. Wilson Company, 1955); *The United States and Asia* by Lawrence H. Battistini (New York: Frederick A. Praeger, 1955); *American-Asian Tensions*, edited by Robert Strausz-Hupé, Alvin J. Cottrel, and James E. Dougherty (New York: Frederick A. Praeger, 1956); *The United States and the Far East*, published under the auspices of The American Assembly (New York: Columbia University, 1956); and *The Meaning of Yalta* by John L. Snell (ed.), Charles F. Delzell, George A. Lensen, and Forrest C. Pogue (Baton Rouge: Louisiana State University Press, 1956). For a report on the Bandung Conference, including the texts of major speeches, see George McTurnan Kahin, *The Asian-African Conference, Bandung, Indonesia, April 1955* (Ithaca: Cornell University Press, 1956).

Convenient introductions to Asian literature and thought are *A Treasury of Asian Literature*, edited by John D. Yohannan (New York: John Day, 1956; also New American Library [Mentor] reprint); *The Wisdom of China and India*, edited by Lin Yu-tang (New York: Random House, 1942); *Buddhism* by Christmas Humphreys (London: Penguin, 1958); and *Buddhist Scriptures*, translated by Edward Conze (London: Penguin, 1959).

There are many journals and bulletins on Asia. The most important are: *The Journal of Asian Studies* and *Pacific Affairs*. Their book reviews and the annual bibliography of *The Journal of Asian Studies* are particularly valuable. Current events in Asia and Africa are digested weekly for handy reference in the *Asian Recorder,* an Indian publication.

AFRICA

An excellent introduction to Africa, readable and with a wealth of photographs, is *Focus on Africa* by Richard Upjohn Light (New York: American Geographical Society, 1944). Another superb visual introduction to African life is *South Africa in Transition* by Alan Paton and Dan Weiner (New York: Scribner, 1956). A stimulating popular account of African history before the colonial period is *The Lost Cities of Africa* by Basil Davidson (Boston: Little, Brown, 1959). A lucid analysis of African life in general is *The African To-day and To-morrow* by Diedrich Westermann (3rd ed., London: Oxford University Press, 1949). A comprehensive survey of the continent, region by region and people by people, is *Africa: Its Peoples and Their Culture History* by George Peter Murdock (New York: McGraw-Hill, 1959). For the story of one African region, the Gold Coast, from ancient times until the present, see *Ghana, A Historical Interpretation* by J. D. Fage (Madison: University of Wisconsin Press, 1959). A brief résumé of African history before and during the Age of Exploration will be found in "Africa in the Days of Vasco da Gama," in J. A. Hammerton (ed.), *Universal World History* (New York: Wise, 1939), vol. VII, pp. 1932–1947. A dated but more detailed and still useful account of African history and foreign inroads is *A History of the Colonization of Africa by Alien Races* by Sir Harry H. Johnston (rev. ed., Cambridge: University Press, 1913). Africa in the Age of Imperialism is covered in Halford Lancaster Hoskins, *European Imperialism in Africa* (New York: Holt, 1930), one of the lucid *Berkshire Studies in European History;* in *The Partition and Colonization of Africa* (Oxford: Clarendon Press, 1922), a collection of readable lectures by Sir Charles Lucas; in Parker Thomas Moon, *Imperialism and World Politics* (New York: Macmillan, 1928); and in Norman Dwight Harris, *Intervention and Colonization in Africa* (Boston: Houghton Mifflin, 1914). Developments in the twentieth century are aptly summarized in *European Colonial Expansion since 1871* by Mary Evelyn Townsend with the collaboration of Cyrus Henderson Peake (Philadelphia: Lippincott, 1941) and especially in *Contemporary Africa; Continent in Transition* by T. Walter Wallbank (Princeton: D. Van Nostrand [an Anvil pocketbook], 1956). A brief glimpse of Africa at the time of World War II, with very useful charts and maps, is presented by R. G. and M. S. Woolbert in *Look at Africa*, no. 43 of the *Headline Series* (New York: Foreign Policy Association, 1943). A more detailed, popular description of contemporary Africa is *Africa, Continent of the Future* by George Edmund Haynes (New York: Association Press, 1951). The pace of change in Africa is so rapid that the political status of Western-controlled regions should be checked in the latest issue of such reference works as *The Statesman's Year Book* (London: Macmillan), *The International Year Book and Statesman's Who's Who* (London: Burke Peerage Ltd.), and *The World Almanac* (New York: New York World-Telegram and The Sun). Among the most forceful literary presentations of major problems in modern Africa are the writings of Alan Paton, notably *Cry, the Beloved Country* (New York: Scribner, 1948), and *Black Hamlet* by Wulf Sachs (Boston: Little, Brown, 1947). The challenge which faces American policy-makers in Africa is discussed in Chester Bowles, *Africa's Challenge to America* (Berkeley: University of California Press, 1956) and in *The United States and Africa*, edited by Walter Goldschmidt under the auspices of The American Assembly (New York: Columbia University Press, 1958). For further study, see Lowell Joseph Ragatz (comp.), *A Bibliography for the Study of African History in the Nineteenth and Twentieth Centuries* (Washington: Paul Pearlman, 1943) and Norbert Mylins, *Afrika Bibliographie 1943–1951* (Vienna: Verein Freunde der Völkerkunde, 1954).

INDIA AND PAKISTAN

The simplest introduction to the history of India and Pakistan is *A Short History of India and Pakistan From Ancient Times to the Present* by T. Walter Wallbank (New York: New American Library [Mentor], 1958). A more detailed, lucid, chronological account of Indian history is *A Short History of India* by W. H. Moreland and Atul Chandra Chatterjee (4th ed., London: Longmans, Green, 1957). Cultural developments receive greater attention in *India, A Short Cultural History* by H. G. Rawlinson (New York: D. Appleton-Century, 1938; republished with minor modifications by Frederick A. Praeger, New York, 1952). The Mogul period, during which the Portuguese arrived, is covered in detail in volume IV of *The Cambridge History of India*, planned by Sir Wolseley Haig and edited by Sir Richard Burn (New York: Macmillan, 1937). British India is examined by Philip Woodruff in *The Men Who Ruled India. The Founders of Modern India*

(New York: St. Martin's Press, 1954) and by H. G. Rawlinson in *The British Achievement in India* (London: William Hodge, 1948). A readable introduction to Indian life and customs is Santha Rama Rau, *This is India* (New York: Harper, 1954). The creation of Pakistan is related by Richard Symonds in *The Making of Pakistan* (London: Faber and Faber, 1950). Relations of the United States with India and Pakistan are analyzed by Phillips Talbot and S. L. Poplai in *India and America* (New York: Harper, 1958).

Indian thought is readily approached through *Sources of Indian Tradition,* edited by Wm. Theodore de Bary (New York: Columbia University Press, 1958) and through *A Source Book in Indian Philosophy,* edited by Sarvepalli Radhakrishnan and Charles A. Moore (Princeton: Princeton University Press, 1957). There is a growing number of paperbacks, among them the following Mentor books: *Song of God: Bhagavad-Gita,* translated by C. Isherwood and Swami Prabhavananda; *The Teachings of the Compassionate Buddha,* edited by Edwin Arthur Burtt; *The Meaning of the Glorious Koran,* translated by Mohammed Marmaduke Pickthall; and *The Upanishads: Breath of the Eternal,* translated by Swami Prabhavananda and Frederick Manchester.

For further study, see *South Asia: A Selected Bibliography on India, Pakistan, Ceylon,* compiled by Patrick Wilson (New York: American Institute of Pacific Relations, 1957).

SOUTHEAST ASIA

A comprehensive account of Southeast Asia from ancient times through the present is D. G. Hall, *A History of Southeast Asia* (New York: St. Martin's Press, 1955). Regional developments since World War II are examined in such specialized works as *The Union of Burma. A Study of the First Years of Independence* by Hugh Tinker (London: Oxford University Press, 1957), *Malaya: A Political and Economic Appraisal* by Lennox A. Mills (Minneapolis: University of Minnesota Press, 1958), and *The Smaller Dragon. A Political History of Vietnam* by Joseph Buttinger (New York: Frederick A. Praeger, 1958). A brief introduction to Southeast Asia after World War II is provided in *Spotlight on Asia* by Guy Wint (New York: Penguin, 1956). Problems facing the United States are analyzed in *Southeast Asia and American Policy* by John P. Armstrong, Foreign Relations Series (Chicago: Science Research Associates, 1959).

For further study, see *Southest Asia: A Selected Bibliography*, compiled by John F. Embree, revised by Bruno Lasker (New York: American Institute of Pacific Relations, 1955, mimeo.).

CHINA .

A simple introduction to Chinese life and history is *The United
States and China* by John King Fairbank (rev. ed., Cambridge: Har-
vard University Press, 1958). A brief, more chronological survey of
Chinese history, with emphasis on material contributions, is *A Short
History of the Chinese People* by L. Carrington Goodrich (3rd ed.,
New York: Harper, 1959). A short, vivid narrative of Chinese history,
with emphasis on personalities, is *The Rise and Splendour of the
Chinese Empire* by René Grousset (Berkeley: University of California
Press, 1953; paperback, 1958). A detailed, chronological account is
The Chinese, Their History and Culture by Kenneth Scott Latourette
(3rd ed., revised, two volumes in one; New York: Macmillan, 1946).
Another standard history is Wolfram Eberhard, *A History of China*
(Berkeley: University of California Press, 1950). A chronologically
less clear but more readable work, which captures the spirit of Chinese
culture, is *China, A Short Cultural History* by C. P. Fitzgerald (London: Cresset Press, 1935; reprinted in the United States by Frederick A. Praeger, New York).

Early Sino-European contacts are related in *Europe and China. A
Survey of Their Relations from the Earliest Times to 1800* by G. F.
Hudson (London: Edward Arnold, 1931). A detailed eye-witness
account of conditions in the Age of Exploration is *China in the Sixteenth Century: The Journals of Matthew Ricci, 1583–1610*, translated
by Louis J. Gallagher (New York: Random House, 1953). Chinese
life and customs in the Age of Imperialism are portrayed by S. Wells
Williams in *The Middle Kingdom* (rev. ed., New York: Scribner, 1904,
1907, 2 vols.). An excellent résumé of developments in the nineteenth
and twentieth centuries is *A History of Modern China* by Kenneth
Scott Latourette (London: Penguin, 1954). A detailed study of the
period is Li Chien-nung, *The Political History of China 1840–1928*,
edited and translated by Ssu-yu Teng and Jeremy Ingalls (Princeton:
D. Van Nostrand, 1956). A highly readable interpretation of the impact of Western imperialism on China is *Revolution in China* by
Charles Patrick Fitzgerald (New York: Frederick A. Praeger, 1952).
Changes under Communism are re-examined by the same author in

Flood Tide in China (London: Cresset Press, 1958). A simple interpretation of Chinese history, past and present, is *China, Confucian and Communist* by Helmut G. Callis (New York: Holt, 1959). A clear statement of the issues confronting United States policy-makers in China is John P. Armstrong, *Chinese Dilemma,* Foreign Relations Series, Experimental Edition (Chicago: Science Research Associates, 1956).

Chinese life is vividly portrayed in fiction. The translations of Chi-chen Wang are especially noteworthy. *Traditional Chinese Tales* and *Contemporary Chinese Stories* (New York: Columbia University Press, 1944) and *Stories of China at War* (London: Geoffrey Cumberlege, 1947) contain the plots of many well-known dramas and longer accounts. *The Dream of the Red Chamber* by Ts'ao Hsüeh-ch'in, also translated by Wang, is perhaps the best literary introduction to China in the Age of Exploration. *Chinese Wit and Humor,* edited by George Kao (New York: Coward-McCann, 1946) is a little anthology of belles lettres.

An eminently readable introduction to Chinese philosophy is *Chinese Thought, From Confucius to Mao Tse-tung* by H. G. Creel (Chicago: University of Chicago Press, 1953; also New American Library [Mentor] reprint). The persistence of ancient thought in modern times is discussed vividly in *Collision of East and West* by Herrymon Maurer (Chicago: Regnery, 1951). An anthology of Chinese thought is being edited by Wm. Theodore de Bary under the title *Sources of the Chinese Tradition* (New York: Columbia University Press, due 1960). A stimulating comparison of Chinese and American motivation and values is *Americans and Chinese: Two Ways of Life* by Francis L. K. Hsu (New York: Henry Schuman, 1953).

For further study, see *A Syllabus of the History of Chinese Civilization and Culture* by L. C. Goodrich and H. C. Fenn (6th ed., New York: The China Society of America, 1958).

KOREA

An excellent introduction to Korea, with useful bibliographical comments for further study, is *Korea's Heritage, A Regional and Social Geography* by Shannon McCune (Tokyo: Charles E. Tuttle, 1956). Foreign relations are examined in more detail in Frederick Nelson, *Korea and the Old Order in Eastern Asia* (Baton Rouge: Louisiana State University Press, 1946).

JAPAN

A lucid, brief history of Japan is *Japan, Past and Present* by Edwin O. Reischauer (2nd ed., New York: Knopf, 1953; reprinted in 1954 and 1956). A more detailed cultural history from antiquity until about the eighteenth century A.D. is *Japan, A Short Cultural History* by G. B. Sansom (rev. ed., New York: Appleton-Century-Crofts, 1943). In *The Western World and Japan. A Study in the Interaction of European and Asiatic Cultures* (New York: Knopf, 1950) Sir George Sansom analyzes European relations with Asia in general during the Age of Exploration and with Japan in particular during the Age of Imperialism. A fascinating account of Japan in the Age of Exploration is *The Christian Century in Japan, 1549–1650* by C. R. Boxer (Berkeley: University of California Press, 1951). Japan during the seclusion period and Russian attempts to reopen the country are described in George Alexander Lensen, *The Russian Push Toward Japan; Russo-Japanese Relations, 1697–1875* (Princeton: Princeton University Press, 1959). The best interpretive history of Japan since the middle of the nineteenth century is *Japan's Modern Century* by Hugh Borton (New York: Ronald Press, 1955). A close-up of the military extremists is given in *The Double Patriots* by Richard Storry (Boston: Houghton Mifflin, 1957). Two pocketbooks on modern Japan should be noted: *Modern Japan: A Brief History* by Arthur Tiedemann (Princeton: Van Nostrand, 1955) and the *Pelican History of Modern Japan* by Richard Storry, scheduled for publication in 1960.

The Japanese national character and Japanese-American relations are discussed in *The United States and Japan* by Edwin O. Reischauer (rev. ed., Cambridge: Harvard University Press, 1957). A brief chronological survey of Japanese-American relations is found in *Japan and America From Earliest Times to the Present* by Lawrence H. Battistini (New York: John Day, 1954). Japanese literature may be approached conveniently through the two-volume *Anthology of Japanese Literature* compiled by Donald Keene (New York: Grove Press, 1955–56). Japanese thought has been gathered together in *Sources of the Japanese Tradition*, edited by Wm. Theodore de Bary (New York: Columbia University Press, 1958). Vivid descriptions of Japanese life are scattered throughout *The Enduring Art of Japan* by Langdon Warner (Cambridge: Harvard University Press, 1952; also Evergreen paperback reprint); *Five Gentlemen of Japan, Portrait of a Nation's*

Character by Frank Gibney (New York: Farrar, Straus, and Young, 1953); *Living Japan* by Donald Keene (New York: Doubleday, 1959); and *Meeting with Japan* by Fosco Maraini, transl. from the Italian by Eric Mosbacher (New York: Viking, 1960).

For further study, see *A Selected List of Books and Articles on Japan in English, French, and German,* compiled by Hugh Borton, Serge Elisséef, William W. Lockwood, John C. Pelzel (rev. ed., Cambridge: Harvard-Yenching Institute, 1954).

INDEX

m = map; thus, 24m refers to the map on page 24.